PAPER
FLOWERS
CHINESE
STYLE

PAPER FLOWERS CHINESE STYLE

Create Handmade Gifts
and Decorations

By Liu Fang and Yue Yunyun

Better Link Press

On page 1
Fig. 1   A slanting work of flower arrangement consisting of handmade paper roses and callas.

On pages 2 and 3
Fig. 2   This work is made of crepe paper whose color has faded from sky gray to azure. The flowers, plump and unrestrained, symbolize auspiciousness. Together with blue-and-white Chinese porcelain, they look perfect on the dinner table or in the hallway.

Bottom
Fig. 3   This bouquet, consisting of Austin roses, buttercups and dahlias, is overflowing with enthusiasm.

On facing page
Fig. 4   These flowers can be made into a wreath for door handle decoration or used as Christmas ornaments.

This book is edited and designed by the Editorial Committee of *Cultural China* series

Text and Photographs: Liu Fang, Yue Yunyun
Translation: Zhao Gang
Cover Design: Wang Wei
Interior Design: Li Jing, Hu Bin (Yuan Yinchang Design Studio)

Copy Editor: Gretchen Zampogna
Editors: Wu Yuezhou, Cao Yue
Editorial Director: Zhang Yicong

Senior Consultants: Sun Yong, Wu Ying, Yang Xinci
Managing Director and Publisher: Wang Youbu

ISBN: 978-1-60220-030-2

Address any comments about *Paper Flowers: Chinese Style* to:

Better Link Press
99 Park Ave
New York, NY 10016
USA

or

Shanghai Press and Publishing Development Company, Ltd.
F 7 Donghu Road, Shanghai, China (200031)
Email: comments_betterlinkpress@hotmail.com

Printed in China by Shenzhen Donnelley Printing Co., Ltd.
1   3   5   7   9   10   8   6   4   2

CONTENTS

CONTENTS

On facing page
Fig. 5   Consisting of sunflowers and eucalyptus leaves, this flower basket looks warm and enthusiastic, rich in rural flavors.

Fig. 6   Arranged in a single-color Chinese vase and decorated with some small wooden vases, the hydrangeas of different colors and density look elegant and unique, adding vitality to corners of your home.

Preface

Fig. 8   A slanting work consisting of blue peonies and wisteria vines shows the line beauty of Chinese flower arrangement.

Paper flowers break free from the restrictions of the flat form and embody three-dimensional beauty. Having become tired of the stereotyped and identical mass-produced products, people in modern society begin to pursue personal tastes and the expression of "self." Paper flowers meet this need perfectly by instilling intellectual beauty into the hustle and bustle of everyday life. They are now used extensively in weddings, shop windows, parties, houses, and gift decoration. As it enjoys fine plasticity, paper is ideal for artistic creation. With different colors and textures, it can be made into beautiful and lifelike flowers of many kinds, which are environmentally friendly, unique, and enduring.

However, to make such a beautiful and romantic flower out of a thin sheet of paper is by no means easy. It requires of the artist profound cultural accumulation, fine aesthetic attainment, as well as exquisite flower-making skills. Flower culture in China has gone through various stages of development, giving rise to a galaxy of flower-making styles.

In March, when flowers bloom gloriously, one may naturally think of some ancient Chinese poems eulogizing flowers, either the elegant and refined lotus flowers in a summer pond, or the fragrant plum blossoms that defy severe cold. For hundreds of years, poets have bestowed various human qualities on flowers. With unique connotations and colors, they are magical wonders worked out by nature. However, cherishing them alone is not enough. We need artistic creations, such as paper flowers, to bring out the dynamism in real flowers.

On facing page
Fig. 7   A Chinese flower basket consisting of hydrangeas, daisies and redbud leaves, with contrasting colors.

Fig. 10   The magnolia has a profound message in Chinese culture. Arranged in a simple black Chinese-style pottery vase, it looks classically natural.

Setting and some other elements help highlight the beauty of paper flowers. A blue-and-white porcelain vase, or simply a coarse earthen flower vase, supplemented by some dead branches of diverse shapes, suffices to make the flower special and unique.

Since Western floral design focuses on flowers' complexity and plumpness and Chinese design on their thinness and brevity, I have been thinking for years about one question: how can we make Chinese elements and Western aesthetic standards set off each other yet remain in good balance? In this book, we have attempted various floral designs that combine Chinese and Western styles and have integrated Western aesthetics into traditional Chinese culture to avoid monotony. The addition of more creative elements into the works has rendered the flowers with a rich post-modern flavor.

This book offers readers basic skills of paper flower making. It enables them to make the listed flowers with their own hands by following the how-to steps and the paper patterns in the appendix. It also helps them to try other possible floral designs. Seeing your own house elegantly decorated with homemade flowers is sure to be pleasant.

A life with flowers is free from worry and is brimming with what is beautiful.

Yue Yunyun

On facing page
Fig. 9   The transparent glass vase sets off the elegant, pure white flowers.

Introduction

The most beautiful things in this world often do not keep long, such as shooting stars, fireworks, and the prettiest moment of a flower.

My love of flowers started when I was very young. Therefore, I can't help feeling melancholy when they wither away. Ten years ago, when I saw paper flowers for the first time, I fell hopelessly in love with them. Since then, I have become addicted to making paper flowers, designing and producing DIY flowers that are as vivid-looking as fresh ones.

After quitting my job four years ago, I started a life center in the ancient town of Huishan in Wuxi, Jiangsu Province, which combines the activities of making flowers and drinking coffee. There, I am face-to-face with paper and flowers every day and the life is simple and good. Teaching my students to make paper flowers, I have become acquainted with many lovers of paper flowers from all walks of life. We work together to create flowers that last forever.

Nothing in this world is easy to obtain, and the handicraft is no exception. Like others, I have visited paper flower masters, learning from them skills of making paper flowers, and have kept thinking and practicing based on what I read and found online. Gradually, I have developed my own theories about what kind of paper is suitable for making different kinds of flowers. For example, thick and tensile paper is ideal for Chinese magnolia flowers with full and fleshy petals, and color-graduated paper is best for hydrangeas. Light, thin, and transparent paper is ideal for plum, apricot, peach, and cherry flower because their petals are of the same quality.

Simple as it may look, flower-making requires constant effort from the learner. Confined to his own field, he can hardly move forward. In recent years, I had been thinking about designing and producing better paper flowers, but to no avail. Then by fortune, I came to know Yue Yunyun, and together with her I have completed this book. Her paper flower works are gentle and grand, exquisite and agile. With her instruction, I have made substantial leaps in my skills.

Unlike Western paper flowers that are rich in color and gorgeous-looking,

On facing page
Fig. 11   The bright-colored paper moth orchids, resembling those adorable dancing butterflies, illuminate and enliven the corner of your windowsill.

the paper flowers in this book borrow the style of Chinese flower arrangement and imitate the charm of asymmetry in natural scenes. They are concise in composition, with fluent lines and refreshing colors. Supported by different flower vessels and other materials, they look poetic and picturesque, embodying the languages of the flowers to the fullest. Used either as home ornaments or simply as gifts, they highlight the reserved and profound Eastern artistic conceptions and at the same time break away from the traditional Chinese style to showcase the unique vitality of life.

Fig. 13   This upright work focuses on displaying the beauty of the lotus flower and leaves, bringing the viewer a sense of coolness in early summer.

The twenty-four kinds of paper flowers in this book are arranged according to the four seasons in a year, six per season, in the order of the twenty-four solar terms. Invented in ancient China, this unique calendar, which has been placed into UNESCO's list of human nonmaterial cultural heritages, reflects the ancient wisdom of the Chinese people. It divides the period of a year into twenty-four points based on the positions of the sun on the ecliptic (as the earth travels around the sun). Since it mirrors the turn of seasons, change of climate, and relations between climate and cyclic biological phenomena, it is still closely related to our modern daily lives. For instance, the forsythia blooms at the Beginning of Spring, heralding the approach of spring; the water lilies are in full blossom during the Great Heat, signifying the hottest days of a year; the chrysanthemums are in bloom during the Cold Dew, indicating the advent of a golden fall; and the Chinese narcissi bloom during the Slight Cold, showing that the weather will become increasingly colder. Assigning a different paper flower to each point in a season can retain the season's most beautiful moment. Though made of paper, these flowers embody the unity of form and spirit.

The appendix contains the patterns of the twenty-four kinds of paper flowers. You may copy these petals on a piece of paper you like or simply photocopy them, then cut these patterns from the paper following the steps in this book, or you can also use the patterns in your own design.

This book is a summary of my experience in making paper flowers of different styles. I would like to present it to the lovers of life and handicrafts.

Liu Fang

On facing page
Fig. 12   The Western-style mintgreen vase, the Chinese-style blue-and-white enamel jars, and the brightly colored hydrangeas supplemented with vigorous tree branches display a unique beauty by clashing with each other.

Chapter One
Characteristics of Chinese Paper Flowers

As early as Emperor Qianlong's reign (1736–1795) in the Qing Dynasty (1644–1911), paper flower making became popular among common folks. For example, the craft of making flowers with rice paper appeared during this time in Yangzhou, Jiangsu Province. During the last years of Emperor Guangxu's reign (1875–1908), the paper flower industry prospered and paper flowers were worn by women as hair ornaments. Today, new types of Chinese-style paper flowers have been developed based on previous experience and styles. Inheriting the quintessence of Chinese traditional floral arrangement, the paper flowers, though man-made, look as natural as real ones. They have forms, but are not restrained by them. They follow the rules of nature in all respects and offer a large space for artistic creation. Generally, Chinese paper flowers embody the following five characteristics.

Fig. 15　This work, consisting of red beans, carnations and roses, forms a contrast between white and red, showing the symmetrical and neat style of Western flower arrangement. However, the red bean branches break the stable sphere-shaped flower arrangement, lending the whole work an infinite upward force.

1. Being Asymmetrical in Composition

Paper flowers in the West are graceful and compact, often pursuing harmony between parts and whole through symmetrical compositions (fig. 15). In contrast, Chinese paper flowers often adopt asymmetrical compositions, displaying the beauty of changes through variation in height, density, looseness, flexibility, and straightness (fig. 14). In his *History of Vases*, Yuan Hongdao (1568–1610) argued that flowers should be arranged in picturesque disorder, resembling their natural postures. Although following

On facing page
Fig. 14　The lightgreen Chinese peony and pinkish white plum blossoms in a Chinese-style blue-and-white enamel vase resemble the graceful beauty of an ancient painting.

Fig. 16   The bonsai, using a dead tree branch decorated with yellow paper-made plum blossoms, gives prominence to the beauty of lines in composition. It looks natural and unrestrained.

the four basic postures of traditional Chinese flower arrangement, i.e., upright, slanting, horizontal, and pedant, Chinese paper flowers are more flexible in composition. They are exquisite and refined, embodying the characteristics of the Orient; they are man-made, but look as natural as real flowers (fig. 16).

2. Emphasizing Beauty of Lines

In his *On Vase Flower Arrangement*, Zhang Qiande discussed the choice of flower branches, saying that a flower with a purely linear branch cannot be used in flower arrangement, since it fails to create an aesthetic feeling. Therefore, beauty of lines is a salient feature of Chinese paper flowers, as the branches, thick or thin, straight or crooked, long or short, solid or gentle, can generate an unlimited number of interests when matched well (fig. 18). In this book, we not only use diversified forms of man-made branches, but also dead branches from nature for their varied postures. Dead branches can either be used to glue the paper flower on or simply as ornaments to create some special artistic effects.

3. Personifying Flowers

In China, especially after the Sui (581–618) and Tang (618–907) dynasties, flowers, trees, and other plants have often been anthropomorphized. For example, in *The Scripture of Flowers*, an ancient Chinese book on flower breeding skills and experience, all the seventy-one kinds of flowers are sequenced based on their grades. Although there were changes in the Song Dynasty (960–1279), ranking flowers has become established as a Chinese tradition. For example, the peony was ranked the topmost among all flowers, named as "Queen of Flowers" later on, and used as the main flower for arrangements in imperial palaces in the Tang Dynasty. It has come to symbolize prosperity, riches and honor today. The lotus flower represents freedom from human desires and passions and a noble spirit because it grows out of mud unsoiled. For this reason, it is often used as a sacrificial flower to Buddha. More interestingly, the combination of different flowers is also bestowed with a beautiful message. For example, the pine, bamboo, and plum are collectively known as "three friends of winter," or a symbol of lasting friendship; the plum, orchid, bamboo, and chrysanthemum as "four gentlemen," and the cypress branch, evergreen, lotus flower, and lily as a symbol of conjugal felicity.

Every season has its flowers, each of which has its own time of blooming, propensity, flower language, and expression. Personifying them or expressing your emotions with them based on their peculiar characteristics of growth, postures, and the diversified messages they carry, will render each flower you make unique in theme (fig. 17).

4. Matching Flower Colors with the Floral Vessel

Just like humans with emotions, colors also have their own characteristics. For example, red, orange, and yellow make people feel warm and are thus known as warm colors. On

Fig. 17   This work, consisting of plum blossoms, orchids, bamboo and chrysanthemums, compares flowers to human beings, showing a profound message.

Fig. 18   This upright flower arrangement consists of roses, sword lilies and gold berries. With its warm colors, it can be arranged on a table to create a sense of tranquility and peace.

Fig. 19 The calliopsis is rich in pastoral flavor. Bold and unstrained, it is ideal for arrangement in a grass-woven floral vessel.

the contrary, blue, green, and purple are cold colors as they make people feel cold. Normally, warm-color flowers are made for chilly autumn or cold winter, while cold-color ones are ideal for warm spring or hot summer as they can reduce the anxiety of the viewer. Either similar or contrasted colors are often put together, as similarity breeds unity through uniformity and contrast generates vivaciousness through changes. However, as can be anticipated, both collocations have their disadvantages. The similar-color collocation tends to be monotonous, and the contrasted-color collocation more complicated, as it needs to take more elements into consideration.

In traditional Chinese flower arrangement, the colors are often light and elegant, although occasionally they may also form a strong contrast. While inheriting this tradition, Chinese paper flowers have sought to make breakthroughs to be peculiar and novel (fig. 19).

The floral vessels in which the flowers are arranged should conform to the flowers in color and temperament. For example, a glass vessel is suitable for the lily, calla, and African daisy as they are clean and pure, a rattan or grass-woven vessel for the garden cosmos and sunflower as they carry a pastoral flavor, and a Chinese-style vessel for the magnolia and camellia as they are brimming with traditional Chinese connotations. When pairing up the flowers and floral vessels, pay attention to the harmony of colors and distinction between what is primary and what is secondary.

5. Integrating a Work into Its Setting

According to *History of Vases* authored by Yuan Hongdao, a scholar's study should be elegantly concise, containing nothing more than a naturally shaped table and a rattan bed, as it is where they read and meditate. The table should be broad and thick, with a fine hand feel. The natural-colored rattan bed should echo the flowers from afar, creating a plain and neat setting. Painted, gilded, or mother-of-pearl inlay furniture should not be used as it is often excessively decorated and does not fit into the general picture. Obviously, traditional Chinese flower arrangement combines multi-sensory beauty and highlights

Fig. 20　Flowers can be used for home decoration. They should be in harmony with the overall setting.

overall harmony of a work.

An enjoyable paper flower work awakens the viewer to Buddhist truth with its natural postures, instills more vitality into the space by capturing a real moment of life through exhibiting the course of growth of the flowers, or strikes an aesthetic chord with the viewer by conveying the owner's artistic inspirations and personal taste. Identifying with the overall setting is the last step of paper flower making. It requires that we are crystal clear about the specific setting in which the work is placed right before we start, and that we incorporate this into the design of the work. On the other hand, the setting can also guide us in our production. Today, Chinese paper flower making, while building itself on traditional floriculture, seeks its own unique styles. Gracefully reserved, natural, and refined, the flowers display a fine fusion between the rhythmic beauty of Oriental paintings and the modern style, satisfying the aesthetic demand of modern days.

The integration between paper flowers and setting can be further extended. The flowers can even serve as ornaments by themselves, such as the frameless picture, bouquet, wall hanging, garland, headdress, wrist flower, window decoration, flower mirror, and flower hanger. New flower-making ideas originate from every moment in life; they are strengthened when fitting in with the setting (fig. 20).

Chapter Two
Preparations

T his chapter introduces the materials and tools needed for making paper flowers. Since paper is the most crucial material, it has been sorted out for detailed introduction. You can choose the materials and tools based on their characteristics and functions and on the specific flower you are going to make.

1. Paper

Since each flower possesses its own unique properties, it is only natural that the paper and its colors be selected according to the specific flower to be made and the creative design in the maker's mind. The commonly used paper includes paper rattan, crepe paper, crepe wrapping paper, float-dye paper, handmade paper, etc. Certainly, all other kinds of paper can also be used to make paper flowers, which sometimes may produce even more interesting effects.

Paper rattans: They are made by twisting a paper strip 10 centimeters in width into a string following seven steps. Rich in color, resilient, and easy to keep, they are used to make the sunflower (page 111) and the camellia (page 157) in this book.

Crepe paper

Paper rattans

On facing page
Fig. 21   A bouquet of brightly colored common peonies symbolizes marital love. It is used as a wedding bouquet.

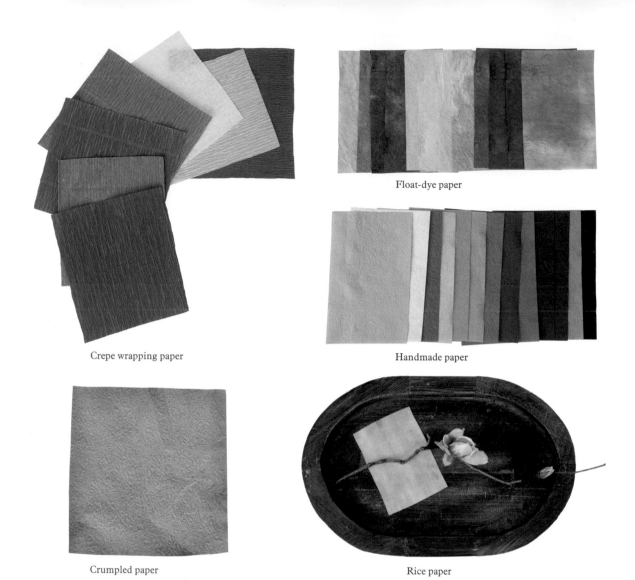

Crepe wrapping paper

Float-dye paper

Handmade paper

Crumpled paper

Rice paper

Crepe paper: It is thin in texture, with its veins resembling those of toilet paper. It is less frequently used for its fragility. In this book, it is only used to make the pomegranate flower (page 93).

Crepe wrapping paper: It is thicker than crepe paper and does not wear easily. Therefore, it is often used to wrap flower bouquets. Fine-grained crepe wrapping paper is ideal for making formative flowers. Most of the flowers in this book are made of this paper.

Float-dye paper: It has irregular dyed grains on its surface and is often used to make paper lanterns or wrapping materials. Flowers made from this paper look natural and beautiful, such as the apricot flower (page 45), the rose (page 51), and winter sweet (page 163) in this book.

Handmade paper: It is resilient and does not fade easily. Compared with the machine-made crumpled paper that is fragile and fades easily, handmade paper is more suitable for paper flower making. In addition, you can also make more creative flowers by dying the white handmade paper based on your design. The paper is used to make the water lily (page 105), the dahlia (page 129), and the sacred bamboo (page 153) in this book.

Rice paper: It is made with the stem pith of a plant named rice paper plant. The pith is taken out of the stem while it is still wet, cut into sections, straightened and dried, and then processed into slightly transparent sheets. This paper is soft, pure white, and malleable. In this book, it is used to make the fine-grained and pure white Yulan magnolia flower (page 57).

Crumpled paper: It is often used to make leaves, such as those of the moth orchid (page 175), the lily of the valley (page 75) and the hydrangea flower (page 99).

Yoshire paper: It is thin and transparent, often used to make the husk of a flower and create a feeling of agility.

Tissue paper: It is used to make the inner core of a bud or baby's breath.

Yoshire paper

Tissue paper

2. Materials

Handmade tape: Unlike ordinary adhesive tapes, handmade tape feels like fabric, is less adhesive, and can be torn apart with hands. It is often used in flower arrangement and the making of artificial flowers. Rich in color and convenient in use, it can be used to make stamens or wrap line rods.

Artificial stamens and berries: Stamens can be made or purchased, and so can small berries.

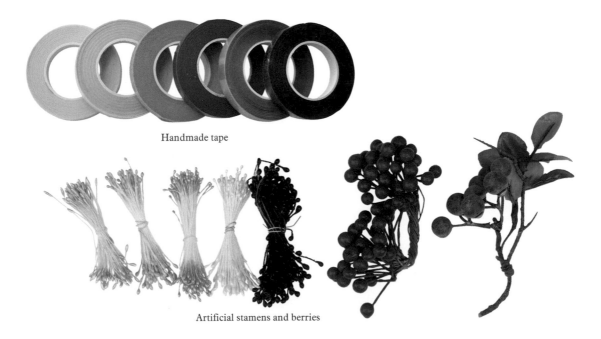

Handmade tape

Artificial stamens and berries

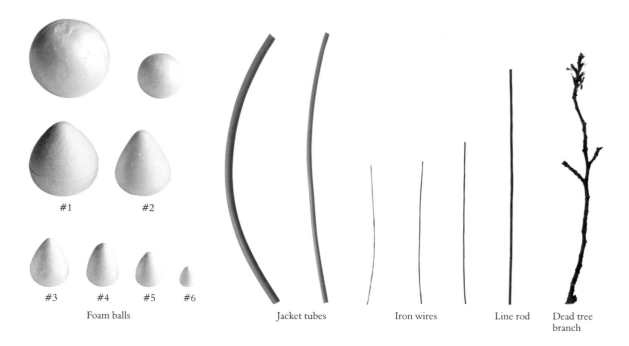

#1

#2

#3 #4 #5 #6

Foam balls

Jacket tubes

Iron wires

Line rod

Dead tree branch

Foam balls: Foam balls are categorized based on the diameters of their bottoms. They are ideal for making flower cores and buds. On the top left corner are some foam balls ranging between #1 and #6. The two round foam balls suit round flowers, such as the Chinese peony and the dahlia. In case there are no foam balls, you can also make buds out of the tissue paper glued together.

Jacket tubes: They are used to thicken the line rod and often serve as the fleshy stalk of such flowers as lotus flower, tulip and hyacinth.

Iron wires: Iron wires fall into different specifications. The bigger the number is, the finer the wire. The common specifications include #26, which is the finest and can often be used to make leaves and smaller flowers; #22, which is medium-sized and can be used to make thinner line rod; and #18, which is thicker and can serve as the line rod directly.

Line rod: Line rods also fall into different specifications and often have a plastic covering. The common ones are #2 line rod, which can serve as the line rods of such flowers as roses and carnations, and #3 and #5 line rods, which are thicker and can be used for bigger flowers like hydrangeas.

Dead tree branch: A more vivid effect can be produced based on the natural shape of the dead tree branch.

3. Tools

Awl: Used to help produce veins on petals or to make holes.

Pliers: Choose a pair of 6-inch stainless steel pliers to bend iron wires.

Scissors: Choose a pair of good-quality and easy-to-use stainless steel scissors. A pair of safety scissors can be chosen for children.

Hot melt glue gun: Often used in quick fixing. Ideal for fixing petals and

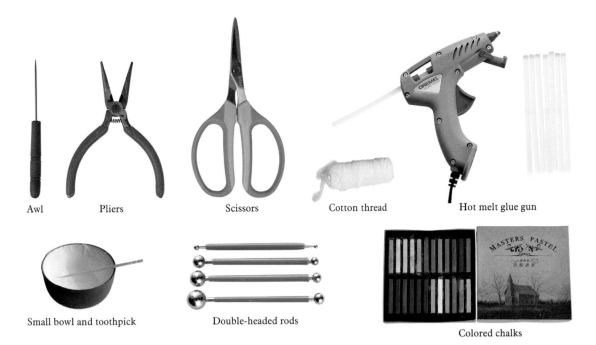

Awl   Pliers   Scissors   Cotton thread   Hot melt glue gun

Small bowl and toothpick   Double-headed rods

Colored chalks

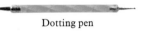

Dotting pen

Glue bottle

Knurling tool

Water-soluble colored pencils

Watercolor pens

Oil-based markers

flowers.

Dotting pen: Used for petal bending for a natural and three-dimensional effect. Ideal for smaller petals.

Double-headed rods: Like the dotting pen, the double-headed rod is used to make the petals look more three-dimensional. It is ideal for bigger petals.

Glue bottle: With white latex inside it, the bottle is mainly used for gluing. It is especially convenient when one applies glue onto a larger area.

Small bowl and toothpick: Put white latex into the small bowl. Pick up a small amount of white latex with the toothpick for pasting at some tender places.

Cotton thread: Used to fix the petal onto a branch by wrapping them together. It is ideal for securing smaller flowers such as jasmine, because the glue, if overused, may affect the shape of the petal.

Knurling tool: With fixed flower patterns, they can be used to produce regularly shaped petals and stamens, such as the stamen of the corn poppy (page 81).

Colored chalks: Used to color the petals and leaves. You can scrape dust down from the chalk with a knife and then dip with a brush and apply them onto the petals and leaves.

Water-soluble colored pencils: For making natural and even color transitions

Watercolor pens: Ideal for painting stamens and dots on petals.

Oil-based markers: Ideal for coloring rice paper or making petals rich in color.

Chapter Three
Basic Techniques and Preservation

Knowing how to handle the major parts of a flower, i.e., petals and leaves, is equivalent to obtaining the key to the gate of the paper flower world. The paper used in flower making is usually highly flexible and ductile so it can be changed or molded in shape by a scissors, a dotting pen or any other appropriate tools. Even if no tools are available, we can create flowers of different shapes with our own hands. In addition, the creation of other necessary components of a paper flower, such as stamens and buds, will be introduced in Chapter Four, for they vary with different kinds of flowers.

The paper flower also requires tender care to remain vivid and beautiful. Therefore, in this chapter, besides teaching you the basic techniques of making petals and leaves, we also offer you tips to maintain paper flowers.

1. Basic Techniques

Using your fingers with dexterity, you can produce petals with a large variety of shapes and a three-dimensional effect. These techniques, such as pulling, pressing, rubbing, pinching, scraping and rolling, can be completely mastered with some practice. The organization of leaves is also very flexible — with imagination and inspiration, you can think of many methods to arrange them. The thickness of flower stems is decided by different flowers, and is not at all hard to learn. Just as no two leaves in the world are exactly the same, no two stamens are identical. Observe flowers in nature carefully and then use these techniques comprehensively, and you can produce completely unique flowers.

Petals
In the following, we will introduce 10 methods of making petals. Using tools and your hands dexterously, you can create petals of different shapes.

On facing page
Fig. 22 These magnolias made of rice paper look authentic. Supplemented with dead branches, they pass for genuine flowers. Arranged with a tea set, they carry a Buddhist mood.

The edge of the petal should be cut round and smooth. Of the two petals in the picture, the chipped one on the left can produce a better effect, but the one on the right has some uneven edges and corners on it, which is not pleasant to the eye.

Petals made of crepe wrapping paper are elastic. You can bulge it out using your fingertips. This method can be used to produce three-dimensional petals, such as those of roses and Chinese peonies.

Produce a wavy effect by pulling the edge of the petal with your fingers in tandem as shown in the picture.

Scrape the edge of the petal with the back of the scissors until it turns up.

Push the dotting pen against your fingertip and scrape the petal until it turns up.

Intertwine the petal around the awl to produce the long and curly shape.

Hold the petal with both hands as shown in the picture. Twist it with force before reopening it to produce fine grains on it.

Scrape the leaf with your fingernail until natural veins appear on it. Use this method to produce veins on petals.

Wrap the petal around the awl and press it toward the end of the awl as shown in the picture. Use this method to produce wrinkles on the petal conveniently.

Hold the end of the petal with one hand, and pull it with force toward the opposite direction with another. Be careful not to pull it apart. Meanwhile, twist the end of the petal to produce vertical veins. Such petals, long and thin, are suitable for dahlias (page 129).

Leaves

In this section, we will introduce three techniques of making leaves based on three types of leaf as examples.

The Single-Layer Method (Dusty Miller Leaf)

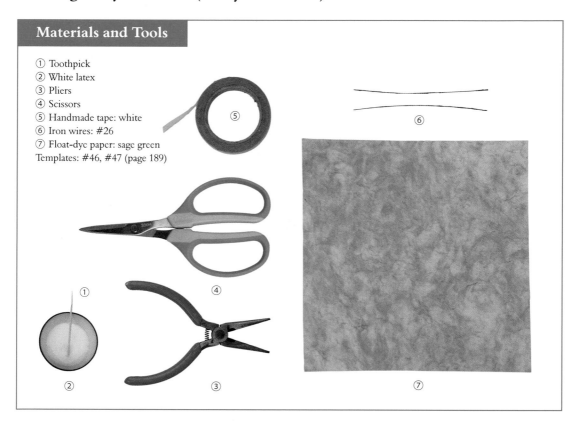

Materials and Tools

① Toothpick
② White latex
③ Pliers
④ Scissors
⑤ Handmade tape: white
⑥ Iron wires: #26
⑦ Float-dye paper: sage green
Templates: #46, #47 (page 189)

How to Make It

1 Cut out the shape of the leaf based on the patterns #46 and #47 on page 189.

2 Cut out leaves of different sizes.

3 Apply white latex to the upper part of the #26 iron wire.

4 Paste the iron wire along the central line of the leaf.

5 Fold the leaf in half, and press it with your finger along the iron wire, so it is securely fixed between the folded leaves.

6 Unfold the leaf after the glue dries up.

7 Cut the white tape into two along the central line.

8 Wrap it around the stalk of the leaf.

9 Follow steps 3 to 8 in treating all the leaves.

10 Scrape the leaves with the back of the scissors until they slightly turn up naturally.

11 Organize all the leaves with the white tape from top to bottom and from small to big.

12 A branch of dusty miller leaves was completed based on the single-layer method.

The Diagonal Method (Eucalyptus Leaf)

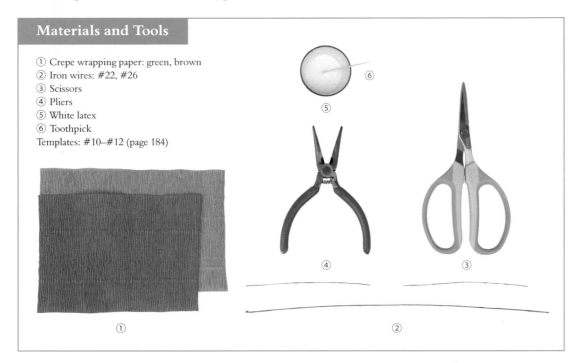

Materials and Tools

① Crepe wrapping paper: green, brown
② Iron wires: #22, #26
③ Scissors
④ Pliers
⑤ White latex
⑥ Toothpick
Templates: #10–#12 (page 184)

How to Make It

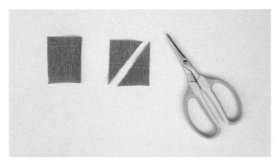

1 Cut a 5-by-5-centimeter square out of the green crepe wrapping paper and then cut it along the diagonal line.

2 Apply white latex onto the hypotenuse of the right-angled triangle.

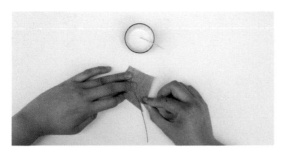

3 Paste the #26 iron wire onto the hypotenuse of one right-angled triangle and then paste another right-angled triangle onto the iron wire as shown in the picture.

4 As is shown in the picture, the veins of the leaf should be in the shape of a tick (√).

5 Cut out some long strips, 0.5 centimeter in width, out of the brown crepe wrapping paper.

6 Pull the elastic strips long and thin.

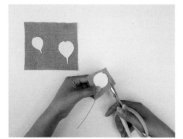

7 Refer to the patterns #10 to #12 on page 184. Cut the shape of a leaf with the iron wire placed along the central line of the leaf patterns.

8 Make several leaves using the above method: some big, some medium-sized, and some small.

9 Apply white latex onto the brown strips and wrap them around the stalks of the leaves.

10 Scrape the leaves with the back of the scissors until they turn up naturally.

11 Treat all the leaves similarly.

12 Wrap the leaves together with the brown tape to form small branches of leaves.

13 Turn the small branches into a big branch by adding the #22 iron wire to it. A branch of eucalyptus leaves based on the diagonal method is thus complete.

The Double-Layer Method (Redbud Leaf)

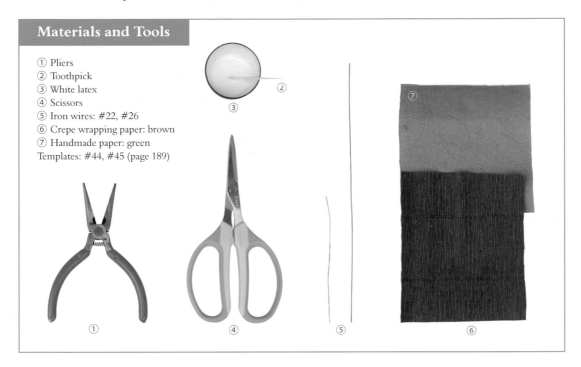

Materials and Tools

① Pliers
② Toothpick
③ White latex
④ Scissors
⑤ Iron wires: #22, #26
⑥ Crepe wrapping paper: brown
⑦ Handmade paper: green
Templates: #44, #45 (page 189)

How to Make It

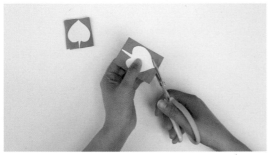

1 Cut out leaves of different sizes based on the patterns #44 and #45 on page 189.

2 Apply white latex to one side of the leaves.

3 Place the #26 iron wire in the middle of a leaf. Paste another leaf of the same size onto this leaf, so that the iron wire is fixed between the two pieces.

4 Treat the big and small leaves in the same way.

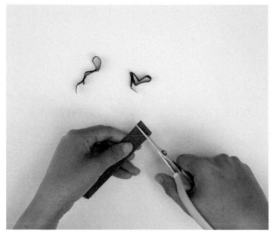

5 Cut some long strips, 0.5 centimeter in width, out of the brown crepe wrapping paper.

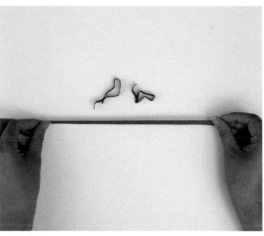

6 Pull the strips open.

7 Apply white latex onto the strips and wrap them around the stalks of the leaves.

8 Scrape veins on the leaves with your fingernail.

9 Leaves completed.

10 Arrange the leaves of different sizes onto the #22 iron wire in picturesque disorder.

11 A branch of redbud leaves was thus completed based on the double-layer method.

Stems

The stem is made by wrapping the iron wire with paper. According to the thickness of the stems, you can either use one iron wire or several wires wrapped together.

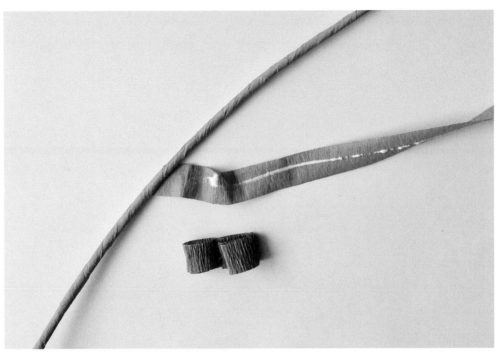

Cut some long strips out of the green crepe wrapping paper, apply glue to them, and wrap them around the wires. Be careful to wrap evenly so that the stems can look natural and proportionate.

2. Preservation and Maintenance

Paper flowers are known as eternal flowers, because they last much longer than fresh flowers. Then, what should we do to preserve and maintain the paper flowers we have made?

- Petals and leaves, once completed, must be allowed to dry in the air thoroughly. They should not be stored in a plastic bag or sealed box before the glue becomes dry, or the iron wire will rust.
- Avoid placing the flower in direct sunlight or in humid places, or it will become deformed or fade in color.
- Brush away the dust on the flower with a soft-hair brush. Use a rubber to erase black traces or finger prints on the flower.
- Paper flowers made of high-quality paper can last as long as two years in natural settings. They will look old if preserved too long.
- To preserve a piece of paper work for a long time, you are recommended to place it into a storage box or mount it.

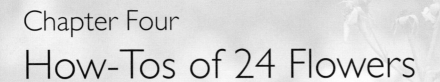

Chapter Four
How-Tos of 24 Flowers

Having learned about the tools and basic techniques of paper flower making, you are now prepared to make paper flowers of your own. In this chapter, using 24 paper flowers as examples, we will show you in great detail how to make flowers of different kinds. The 24 flowers, six in each season, correspond to the 24 solar terms in China and to their distinctive temperaments respectively. Come and learn to decorate your home with these adorable paper flowers.

Fig. 23   In this basket are arranged handmade Chinese peonies, hydrangeas and peonies, which, bathed in the same blessings of heaven and earth, can almost pass for real flowers, creating tranquility and peace.

1. The Forsythia

After a spring shower, while other flowers are still in dead sleep, clusters of forsythia have come into sight. The trumpet-shaped flowers are in full blossom, as if heralding the advent of spring with a concert, bringing out the vitality of the earth with their fragrance. They are loved by many people for their faint yet elegant fragrance, their gorgeous beauty, and their strong adaptability. They are also the painter's favorite as they, either thick or slight in color, can set off the air of spring perfectly. In traditional Chinese medicine, the fruits of forsythia can serve to clear away heat and toxic materials.

The language of the flower: eternal love.

Lichun (Beginning of Spring): February 3–5

Lichun is the 1st solar term according to the 24 terms of the year. Since the Qin Dynasty (221–206 BC), it has been taken as the start of spring, which reminds people of warmth, chirping birds, blooming flowers, sowing and growth. In early spring, while other flowers are still asleep, the forsythia starts to blossom, bringing an air of spring.

Materials and Tools

① Dead tree branch
② Handmade tape: brown
③ Iron wires: #18, #26
④ White latex
⑤ Toothpick
⑥ Scissors
⑦ Plaster stamens
⑧ Dotting pen
⑨ Colored pencil (brown)
⑩ Crepe wrapping paper: green
⑪ Handmade paper: yellow, green
Templates: #1–#4 (page 184)

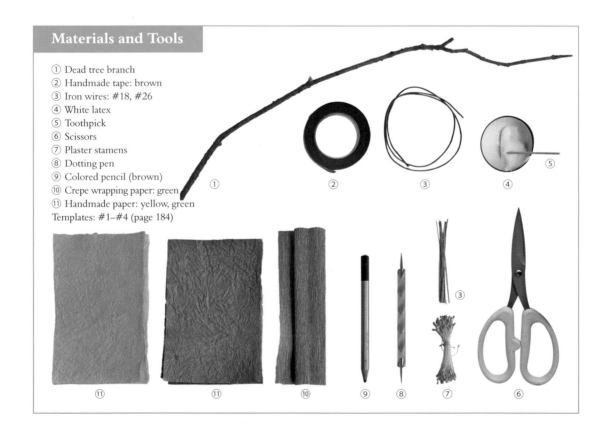

How to Make It

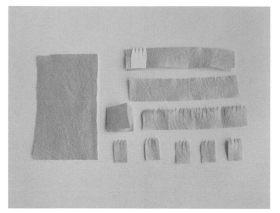

1 Cut some slips out of the yellow handmade paper based on the pattern #1 on page 184; these will be used to make forsythia petals.

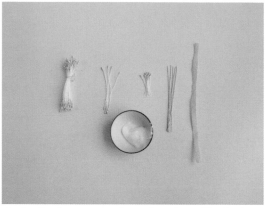

2 Cut the plaster stamens in two from the middle. Cut the yellow paper into slender strips.

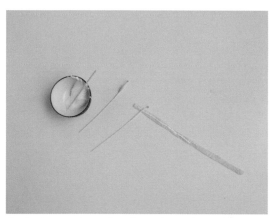

3 Apply some glue to the yellow strips, and wrap the stamens onto the #26 iron wire. Be careful to expose the ball on the top of the stamens.

4 Keep wrapping where the stamen and the iron wire meet until it becomes olive-shaped.

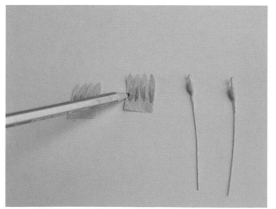

5 Use the colored pencil to tint the yellow slips from step 1 brown.

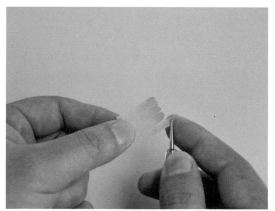

6 Place the slip on your fingertip, press the dotting pen against your fingertip, and make the slip curve naturally by pressing, scraping and rolling it.

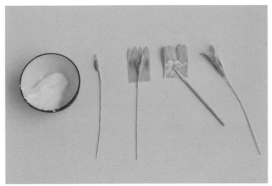

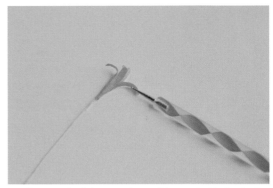

7 Apply some glue to the bottom of the slip and place the stamen in its middle. Then wrap the slip evenly around the stamen. Pinch the bottom tightly to create the petal of the forsythia.

8 Scrape and roll the outer layer of the petal with the dotting pen, making the petal bend downward. It is better to leave the scraping traces so that the petal looks more natural. This way, a branch of the forsythia is finished.

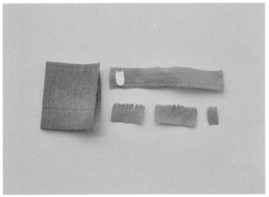

9 Cut some shapes of calyx out of the green crepe wrapping paper based on the pattern #4 on page 184, and scrape and roll their fringes with the scissors so that the calyxes curve naturally.

10 Apply some glue to the bottom of the calyx and wrap it evenly around the bottom of the flower.

11 Make some leaves with the green handmade paper. First, cut some rectangle slips of appropriate sizes out of the green paper based on the patterns #2 and #3 on page 184. Then, apply some glue to the #26 iron wire, place it on the center line of the slip, fold the slip along the iron wire, and fix them tightly together by pinching the iron wire. Finally, unfold the slip after the glue dries, and cut the shape of a leaf out of it based on the patterns in the appendix.

12 Make more flowers and leaves for later use.

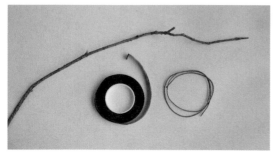

13 Prepare some dead branches you like or a #18 iron wire and some brown tape, which will be used to make the flower branch.

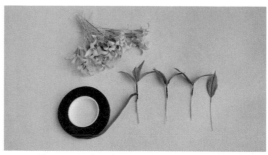

14 Glue two or three leaves together with the brown tape.

15 Fasten the flowers and leaves in appropriate density onto a dead branch with the brown tape.

16 Glue two or three flowers together with the brown tape.

17 Organize the flowers and leaves in appropriate density along the branch from top to bottom.

18 Make a furcated flower branch with a thinner branch based on the method of making the main flower branch.

19 Fasten the furcated branch onto the main flower branch with the tape.

20 Thus a branch of forsythia is complete.

2. The Apricot Flower

The apricot flower is white touched with red, looking like the subtle skin of a girl—pure, gentle and beautiful. The earliest record about this flower is found in 221 BC, which shows that it has been cultivated in China for about 3,000 years. Emperor Huizong (1802–1135) of the Song Dynasty once composed a poem in praise of the beauty and fragrance of the apricot flower. In Chinese tradition, the apricot flower is listed as the Goddess for February, showing its status in the flower world.

The language of the flower: shyness of girls.

Yushui (Rain Water): February 18–20

Yushui is the 2nd solar term according to the 24 terms of the year, meaning it begins to rain. In the Yellow River area where the 24 solar terms originated, after *Yushui*, there is gradually less snow but more rain. It is in this period of time, apricot flowers begin to blossom.

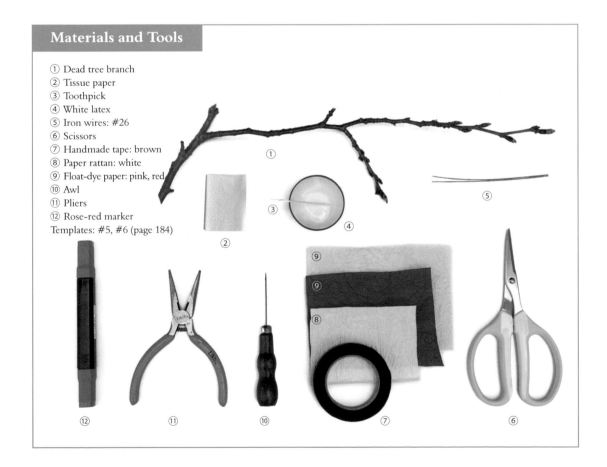

Materials and Tools

① Dead tree branch
② Tissue paper
③ Toothpick
④ White latex
⑤ Iron wires: #26
⑥ Scissors
⑦ Handmade tape: brown
⑧ Paper rattan: white
⑨ Float-dye paper: pink, red
⑩ Awl
⑪ Pliers
⑫ Rose-red marker
Templates: #5, #6 (page 184)

How to Make It

1 Cut some petal shapes out of the pink float-dye paper based on the pattern #5 on page 184.

2 Wrap the petal around the awl, and press it toward its lower end to produce some fine veins.

3 Make the petal look three-dimensional with your fingers.

4 Take out the white paper rattan with the specification of 2 by 4 centimeters. Apply white latex onto it and fold it in half along the longer edge.

5 Cut out fine fringes on one edge of the rattan paper.

6 Bend an end of the #26 iron wire into a hook with pliers.

7 Hook a small part of the fringes and then clamp them tightly together.

8 Apply white latex onto the bottom of the rattan paper.

9 Make the flower core by wrapping the hook tightly with the paper. Paint the shapes of pollen on the top with the marker.

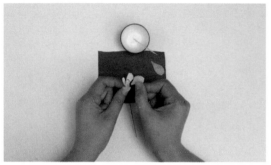

10 Apply white latex onto the bottom of the petals and paste them one after another around the flower core.

11 Paste five petals around the flower core in picturesque disorder.

12 Cut a long strip with a width of 0.5 centimeter out of the tissue paper, hook it on one end with the #26 iron wire, and apply white latex to the strip.

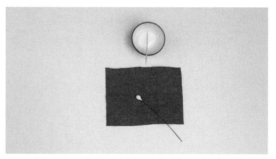

13 Wrap the strip around the end with the hook on it until it becomes the shape of a soybean.

14 Cut a square strip of 3 by 3 centimeters out of the pink float-dye paper, apply white latex onto it, and wrap it around the tissue paper to produce a flower bud.

15 Cut the shape of a calyx out of the red float-dye paper based on the pattern #6 on page 184.

16 Apply some white latex on it and then wrap it at the bottoms of the flower and the bud.

17 Make several flowers and buds.

18 Cut the brown tape into two as shown in the picture.

19 Fasten the buds and flowers in twos and threes with the tape.

20 Then arrange them in turn onto the dead tree branch.

21 A branch of white apricot flowers touched with red is thus complete.

3. The Rose

The rose blooms fragrantly and luxuriantly in spring, with different flower shapes and colors, showing the vitality of earth when spring returns. In one of his poems, Du Mu (803–853), a well-known poet in the Tang Dynasty, eulogized the rose for its gentle leaves, profuse flowers and pleasant smell. In addition, the rose is a symbol of love in China. The red roses are passionate yet graceful and restrained, like man and woman deep in love, whose affection to each other is shown in whispers and smiles.

The language of the flower: I miss you.

Jingzhe (Waking of Insects): March 5–7

Jingzhe is the 3rd solar term according to the 24 terms of the year. By then, the temperature has risen, the soil has begun to thaw, and the roaring spring thunders have awakened the hibernating animals and insects. During this time, in most of the rural areas in China, people have started spring ploughing. The rose, like a beauty who has been asleep all winter, now begins to wake up.

Materials and Tools

① Tape: green
② White latex
③ Toothpick
④ Yellow marker
⑤ Scissors
⑥ Pliers
⑦ Iron wires: #26, #22
⑧ Float-dye paper: pink, green, milk white
Templates: #7–#9 (page 184)

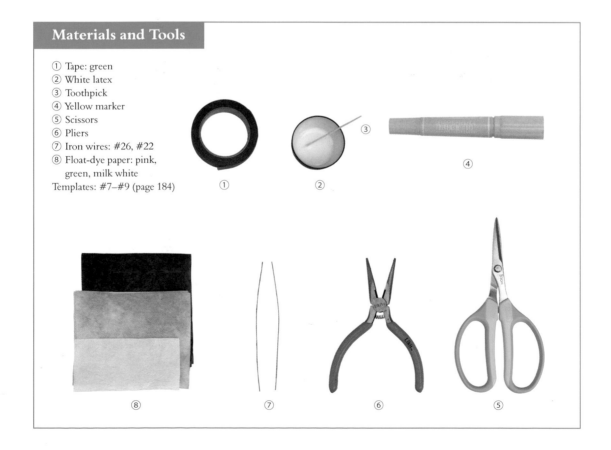

How to Make It

1 Cut a rectangular strip out of the float-dye paper, 1.5 by 3 centimeters. Cut out fine, dense fringes with the scissors on one of the longer edges of the strip.

2 Bend one end of the #26 iron wire into a hook. Hook a small part of the rectangular strip and apply white latex onto its bottom.

3 Wrap the strip onto the hook as the flower core.

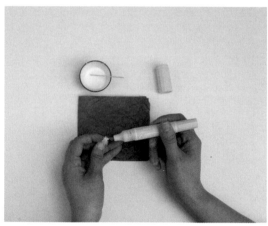

4 Paint the pollen on top of the stamen with the yellow marker.

5 Cut a square strip out of the pink float-dye paper, 4.5 by 4.5 centimeters. Fold it as shown in the picture and then cut down the part marked as red based on the pattern #7 on page 184. Unfold what is cut down and you get a shape consisting of five petals.

6 Refold the petal and cut a small opening at its tip.

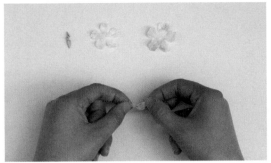

7 Twist the petal before unfolding it. Adjust it to make it more petal-like. Make more such petals for later use.

8 Apply white latex around the circular hole in the center of the petal.

9 Pass the stamen from step 4 through the circular hole in the petal, and pinch them tight to form a flower.

10 Apply white latex onto more petals and paste them one by one at the bottom of the petal from step 9. A flower needs three to five petals.

11 Cut a long strip, 0.5 centimeter wide, out of the tissue paper.

12 Bend one end of the #26 iron wire into a hook with the pliers. Hook a small section of the long strip and then clamp them tightly with the pliers.

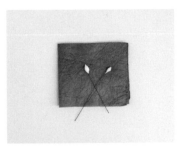

13 Apply white latex onto the long strip and wrap it around the iron wire. Make it olive-shaped with your fingers.

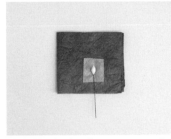

14 Apply white latex onto one side of the pink float-dye paper and place the olive-shaped end of the iron wire in the center of the paper.

15 Twist the float-dye paper from both ends as shown in the picture to produce the shape of a bud.

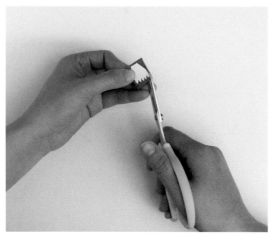

16 Cut some calyxes out of the green float-dye paper based on the pattern #8 on page 184.

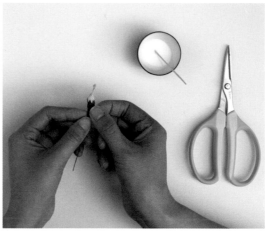

17 Apply white latex onto one side of the calyx and wrap it around the bottom of the bud.

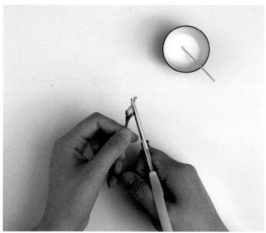

18 Cut the redundant part on the top of the bud with the scissors.

19 Apply white latex evenly onto the calyx and paste it at the bottom of the bud and the flower.

20 Cut the green tape in half along the central line.

21 Wrap the tape around the branches of the flower and the bud.

22 Make more flowers and buds of varied sizes.

23 Apply white latex onto the lower half of the green float-dye paper with the specification of 4 by 8 centimeters. Fix the #22 iron wire in the center of the lower half of the paper and then fold the paper in half so that both sides are pasted together. Cut the shape of a leaf out of the paper based on the pattern #9 on page 184.

24 Scrape some veins on the leaf with your fingernail. Make more leaves for later use.

25 Cut the green tape in half along the central line. Fasten 3 to 5 leaves together with the tape onto the iron wire. Make more groups of leaves for later use.

26 Fasten the flowers, buds and leaves together with the green tape.

27 A bunch of blooming roses is complete.

4. The Yulan Magnolia Flower

Growing Yulan magnolia flowers has had a long history in China. The flowers, often found in front of pavilions, have been loved by Chinese people since time immemorial. They are either jade-white, elegant and graceful, or white touched with purple, unique and charming. They are not only beautiful, but are endowed with an admirable spirit, since, delicate as they look, they bloom gorgeously against the chill in late winter and early spring.

The language of the flower: pure and noble.

Chunfen (Vernal Equinox): March 20–21

Chunfen is the 4th solar term according to the 24 terms of the year. This period from the Waking of Insects (*jingzhe*) to Vernal Equinox is famous for flower appreication. It is also when Yulan magnolia flowers are in full bloom.

Materials and Tools

① Scissors
② Iron wires: #24
③ Crepe wrapping paper: pink, green, brown
④ Gracefully shaped dead tree branch
⑤ Dry towel
⑥ Tweezers
⑦ Handmade tape: brown
⑧ Toothpick
⑨ White latex
⑩ Rice paper slips
⑪ Face tissue
⑫ Small watering can
⑬ Oil marker pen (purple-red)
Templates: #16–#21
(page 185)

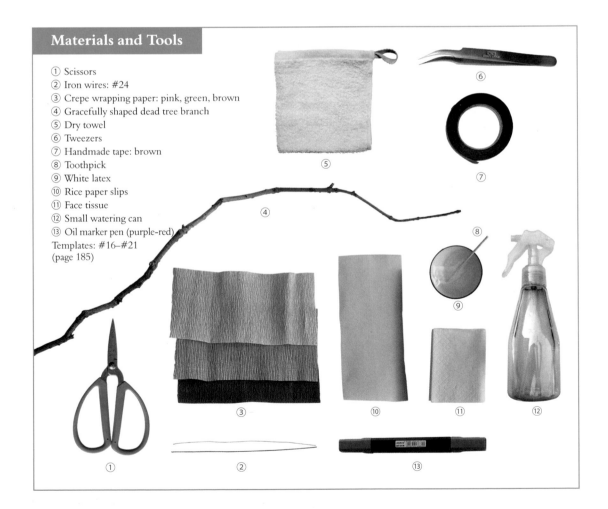

How to Make It

1 Make stamens with the pink and green crepe wrapping paper. Cut out two long, jagged paper strips based on the pattern #16 on page 185, one green and the other pink.

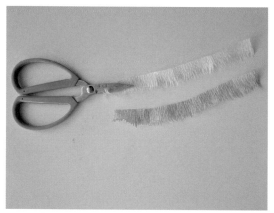

3 Bend the indentions on the pink paper strip with the back of the scissors.

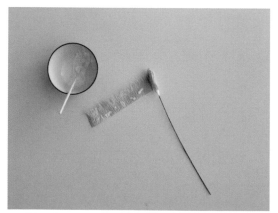

5 Wrap the green indented paper around the tissue strip, with the indentions turning upward and bending inside.

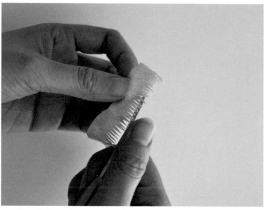

2 Bend the indentions on the green paper strip with the back of the scissors.

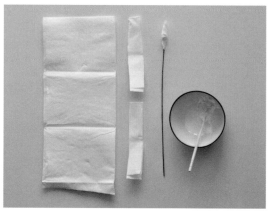

4 Cut the face tissue into strips. Apply some glue to one side of the strip and wrap it around an end of the iron wire in the shape of an olive.

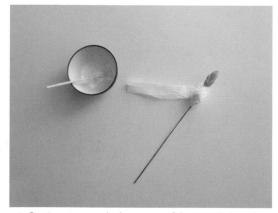

6 Continue to wrap the lower part of the green indented paper with face tissue applied with white latex until it becomes ball-shaped.

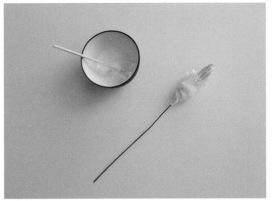

7 Wrap the pink indented paper around the ball, with the indentions turning upward and bending outward.

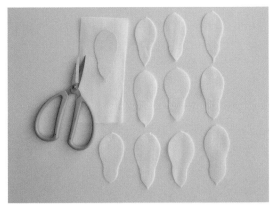

8 Follow the petal patterns #17 to #19 on page 185 and cut nine petals out of the rice paper, three bigger, three medium, and three smaller.

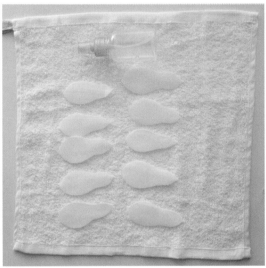

9 Pure, soft, and refined in texture, rice paper is ideal for making hand-painted petals. Before a petal is colored, cushion its bottom with a dry towel and moisten it with a small watering can.

10 While the petal is moist, use a pair of tweezers to stabilize its bottom, and use a purple-red marker pen to paint it from bottom up. Petals treated this way do not fade easily. Follow this process closely to make sure the coloring is natural.

11 Here are the nine colored petals.

12 Bend the petal slightly while it is still moist to create a three-dimensional effect.

13 Curl both sides of the petal top carefully with the back of the scissors.

14 Hold the bottom of the petal with one hand, and twist and then release it with another to make it more natural-looking.

15 Follow steps 12 to 14 in making nine petals, three bigger, three medium, and three smaller. External petals can also curl in the opposite direction.

16 Apply some white latex to the bottom on one side of the petal and paste the three smaller petals evenly onto the stamen completed in step 7.

17 Make sure the petal bottoms are pasted together evenly, without being wrinkled.

18 Paste the three medium-sized petals between the three smaller petals.

19 Make sure that the three medium-sized petals are pasted firmly and evenly at the bottom.

20 Paste the three bigger petals between the three medium-sized petals. Make sure that they are even at the bottom.

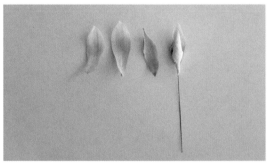

21 Bend the external petals outward to mimic a blooming flower.

22 A bird's-eye view of the flower.

23 Cut out four smallest petals based on the pattern #20 on page 185 and use them to make flower buds. Make the structure of the bud by wrapping one end of the iron wire with face tissue based on step 4. Then enclose it with the four petals.

24 Cut two calyxes out of the brown crepe wrapping paper based on the pattern in the appendix. Twist them before unfolding them.

25 Paste the two calyxes one after another onto the sides of the flower bud, one in a taller position than the other to achieve naturalness.

26 Cut the shape of leaf out of the green crepe wrapping paper based on the pattern #21 on page 185. Twist and then unfold the leaf. Apply white latex to an iron wire and then paste it in the middle of the leaf. Use this method to make another leaf.

27 Put together the dead tree branch, brown crepe wrapping paper slips, white latex, etc. for the final steps.

28 Fasten together the two leaves and the magnolia flower branch by wrapping the brown crepe wrapping paper with white latex on it around them.

29 Fasten the flower bud onto the dead tree branch with the brown handmade tape.

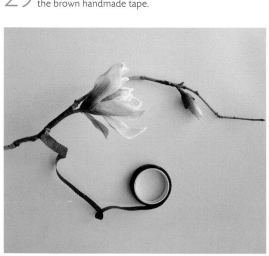

30 Fasten the flower onto the lower part of the dead tree branch with the brown handmade tape.

31 Thus a Yulan magnolia flower rich in Chinese flavor is complete.

5. The Dogwood Blossom

"A lonely stranger in a strange land I'm cast, sore sick for my dears on every festive day. By now my brothers must some heights have passed, but a dogwood wearer missing'll damp the play." This poem by Wang Wei (701?–761) in the Tang Dynasty not only expresses the homesickness of a traveler in a faraway land, but also describes the time-honored tradition of Chinese people wearing dogwood branches and ascend a height for a distant view. It was believed that the dogwood was capable of warding off ill luck and diseases and symbolized longevity, so the Double Ninth Day was later designated as the day for the elderly, as double ninth in Chinese carries the auspicious meaning of being forever or permanent. The dogwood blossom is concise in pattern, elegant, and refreshing. Its fruit is also a common Chinese herbal medicine that warms the liver and tonifies the kidney. Therefore, the plant boasts both appreciation and practical values.

The language of the flower: peace and harmony.

Qingming (Pure Brightness): April 4–6

Qingming is the 5th solar term according to the 24 terms of the year. The Qingming Festival in China started about 2,500 years ago in the Zhou Dynasty (1046 BC–256 BC). It is the time when Chinese people pay respect to their ancestors by sweeping their tombs. The dogwood blossom, which symbolizes homesickness, also blooms during this time.

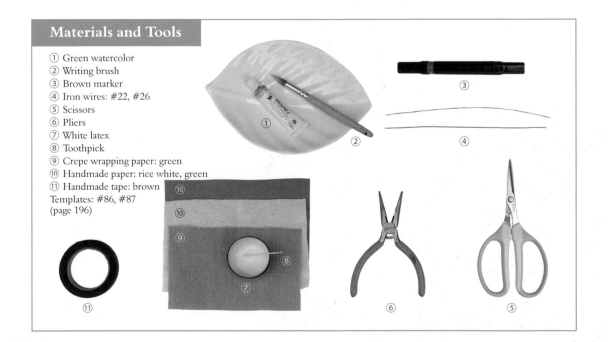

Materials and Tools

① Green watercolor
② Writing brush
③ Brown marker
④ Iron wires: #22, #26
⑤ Scissors
⑥ Pliers
⑦ White latex
⑧ Toothpick
⑨ Crepe wrapping paper: green
⑩ Handmade paper: rice white, green
⑪ Handmade tape: brown
Templates: #86, #87
(page 196)

How to Make It

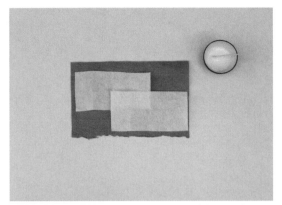

1 Cut two 6-by-12-centimeter strips out of the rice white handmade paper.

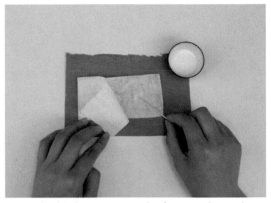

2 Apply white latex onto one side of a strip and paste the two strips together face-to-face.

3 Scrape the strip flat using a supplementary tool (e.g. a business card or a cardboard).

4 Fold the double-layer strip along the longer edge twice. Cut four petals out of it based on the pattern #87 on page 196.

5 Dilute the dense green watercolor by adding some water into it. Paint the petals light green from bottom up.

6 Dot the openings at the top of the petals several times with the brown marker.

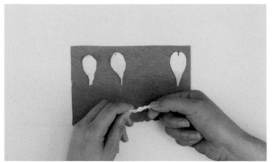

7 Twist the petals and then unfold them, which will produce natural veins on them.

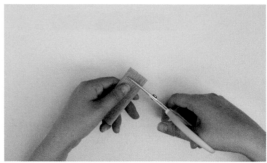

8 Cut a long strip with the specification of 1.5 by 20 centimeters out of the green crepe wrapping paper.

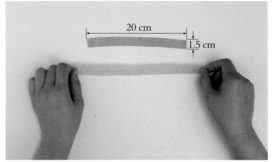

20 cm

1.5 cm

9 Pull the long elastic strip open.

10 Apply white latex onto half of the strip.

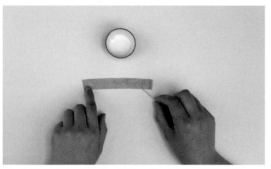

11 Repeat step 10 after folding the strip in half. Fold it again to form a four-layer strip.

12 Cut dentate fringes 2 millimeters in width evenly.

13 Rub the fringes into strands with your fingers.

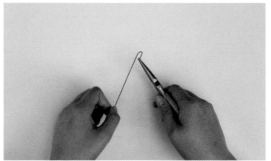

14 Bend the top of the #22 iron wire into a hook.

15 Hook a small section of the fringes and apply white latex below the fringes.

16 Wrap the hook with the strip to form the core of the flower.

17 Apply white latex onto the bottoms of the petals and paste them in turn around the core.

18 The four petals should be distributed evenly.

19 Wrap the iron wire below the flower with the brown tape.

 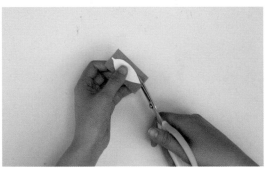

20 Make more flowers for later use.

21 Cut some leaves out of the green crepe wrapping paper based on the pattern #86 on page 196.

22 Apply white latex onto the upper part of the #26 iron wire.

23 Place the iron wire along the central line of the leaf.

24 Fold the leaf into half, press the iron wire tightly before releasing it, and make sure the iron wire is buried inside.

25 Cut the brown tape into two along the central line.

26 Wrap it around the iron wire at the bottom of the leaf.

27 Fasten some of the leaves together in pairs with the tape.

28 Add the #22 iron wire into the flower and leaves and fix them together with the tape.

29 A graceful branch of dogwood blossoms is thus complete.

6. The Chinese Peony

The Chinese peony is one of the six most well-known flowers in China, the rest being the plum, orchid, chrysanthemum, lotus flower, and peony. Graceful in look, lovely in pattern, and voluptuous in color, it boasts great ornamental value. What's more, the Chinese peony is also rich in cultural connotations. Known from the ancient time as flower of love, it has become a symbolic flower to be offered on the traditional Chinese Valentine's Day (July 7). In ancient China, lovers often gave each other a peony to show their mutual affection and the reluctance to leave each other, as is found in *The Book of Songs*, the oldest Chinese poetry, lad and lass in love give each other a Chinese peony. This bunch of pink Chinese peonies, like a bashful girl in love, displays reserved romance.

The language of the flower: already having a lover in one's heart.

Guyu (Grain Rain): April 19–21

Guyu is the 6th solar term according to the 24 terms of the year and the last term in spring. It means that spring shower nurtures grains, as this is a time when the freshly planted seedlings and crops are in urgent need of rainwater. From this time on, Chinese peonies, known as God of Flowers, will begin to bloom.

Materials and Tools

① Crepe wrapping paper: deep pink, light pink, green
② Pliers
③ Scissors
④ White latex
⑤ Toothpick
⑥ Iron wire: #18
Templates: #22–#27 (page 186)

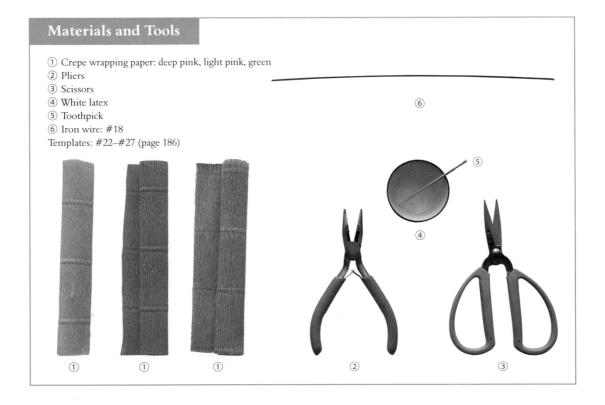

How to Make It

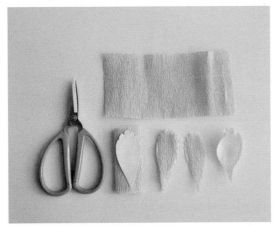

1 Follow the pattern #22 on page 186 to cut some small inner petals out of the pink crepe wrapping paper for later use.

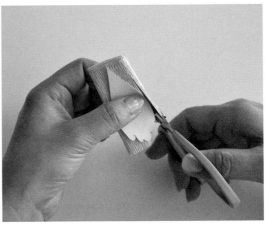

2 Make the petals plump in shape and smooth at the edge.

3 Use your finger pad to create a three-dimensional effect by making each of the petals swell out in the middle.

4 These are a number of inner petals after being treated.

5 Pick up some white latex with a toothpick and apply it at the end of each inner petal to form a combination of three to five petals.

6 Slightly roll the end of the petal combination with your fingers into a long and narrow strip, so that the petals stick more together at the end. Repeat step 5 to make more such petal combinations. The picture shows the final effect.

7 Follow the pattern #23 on page 186 and cut bigger external petals out of the deep pink crepe wrapping paper.

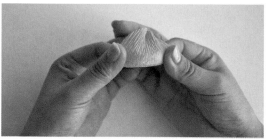

8 Follow step 3 to create a similar bulging three-dimensional effect with your finger pad.

9 Carefully make the petal neat and well-spaced with your fingers. The petal should look plump, smooth and natural at the edge.

10 Repeat step 9 and make each petal plump and three-dimensional.

11 These are a number of bigger external petals after being treated.

12 Wrap a layer of crepe wrapping paper strips with the same color as the inner petals around one end of the iron wire.

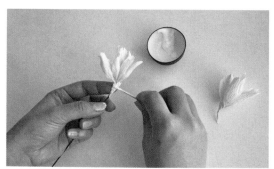

13 Paste the inner petal combinations on the wrapped end of the rod.

14 Having pasted all the inner petal combinations onto the rod, apply some glue to the inside of the petals that are close to the rod and squeeze them tightly between your fingers, so the petals are fixed to the rod more securely.

15 Apply some glue to the inside of the bigger petals at the end and paste them outside the smaller petals.

16 Surround the smaller petals with three layers of slightly overlapping bigger petals inside out. Each layer should be about 1 mm lower than the previous layer to create a sense of hierarchy. Add more layers of bigger petals if a fuller flower pattern is needed.

17 Here is the back of the flower with overlapping petals.

18 Apply some white latex to the inside of the petal, close to the iron wire, and squeeze them tightly together with your fingers, so that the flower is fixed more securely onto the wire.

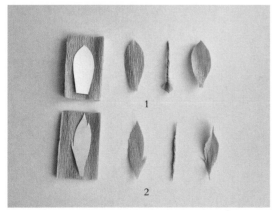

19 Cut two calyxes, shape 1 and shape 2, out of the green crepe wrapping paper based on the patterns #24 and #25 on page 186. Twist and then unfold them for a more natural effect.

20 Cut out three calyxes of either shape and apply some white latex onto their back sides.

21 Paste the three calyxes from shape 1 hierarchically and from inside out onto where the iron wire and the petals meet. Don't paste the tips of the calyxes onto the petals completely. Instead, make them slightly turned up to achieve a more natural effect.

22 Paste the three calyxes from shape 2 between the calyxes from shape 1 in a slightly outward position, so that they look much longer.

23 Follow the pattern #27 on page 186 to cut out leaves. Twist the leaves before unfolding them, so they look more natural. Then cut out a rectangle from the green crepe wrapping paper based on the pattern in the appendix and twist the rectangle into a long, narrow strip to serve as the leafstalk. Fasten together the leaves and leaf stalk using slips of crepe wrapping paper with white latex on them.

24 Cut the crepe wrapping paper into strips by following the pattern #26 on page 186, pull them out, and apply glue to one side.

25 Fasten the leaf stalks onto the iron wire with the paper strips. Wrap the iron wire with several layers of paper strips to make it thicker.

26 A Chinese peony is thus complete.

7. The Lily of the Valley

Lilies of the valley are small but full, snow white, and sweetly scented. Hanging down heavily from the branches, they resemble strings of pure white wind bells tinkling in the breeze. They have a beautiful Chinese name, Enduring Sweetheart, for it is believed that if you sprinkle the perfume made from this flower onto your sweetheart, they will remain loyal to you forever. Though often growing in remote valleys, forests, or deep mountains, they still bloom gloriously, like noble-minded gentlemen who never bend to poverty.

The language of the flower: return of happiness.

Lixia (Beginning of Summer): May 5–7

Lixia is the 7th solar term according to the 24 terms of the year and the 1st solar term in summer. It means the beginning of summer. After that, the region south of the Yangtze River officially enters the rainy season, with increased rainfall and more rainy days. This is exactly the time lilies of the valley are in blossom. The plant is short, but the flowers are elegant and fragrant.

Materials and Tools

① Crumpled paper: green
② Crepe wrapping paper: green, milk white
③ Yoshire paper: brown
④ Toothpick
⑤ Foam balls: #1, #2
⑥ Iron wires: #18, #26
⑦ Ball-headed rods
⑧ Paper tape: yellow
⑨ Scissors
⑩ Pliers
⑪ White latex
Templates: #28–#31 (page 187)

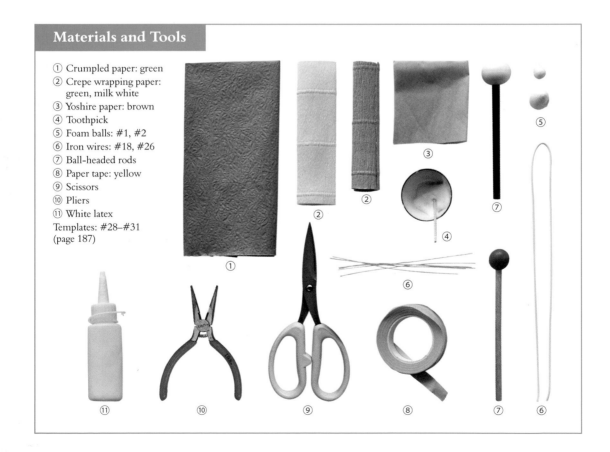

How to Make It

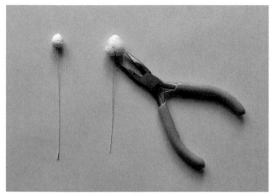

1 Pass the #26 iron wires through the two types of foam ball buds and secure them with the pliers.

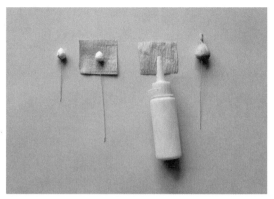

2 Cut a rectangular slip out of the green crepe wrapping paper, big enough to wrap the foam ball. Apply some white latex to the slip and wrap the foam ball with it. Pinch the top and bottom of the slip with your fingers to make them fit tightly.

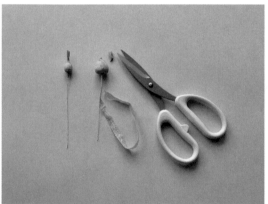

3 Cut the redundant part on the top with the scissors. Cut a long strip out of the green crepe wrapping paper, apply some white latex to it, and wrap it around the iron wire. This way, the two buds, one big and one small, are complete.

4 Cut a section from the yellow tape and wrap it around one end of the #26 iron wire until it becomes olive-shaped. Pinch both ends of the olive with your fingers until it looks like a stamen. Make more stamens for later use.

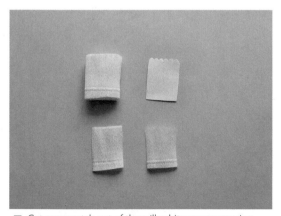

5 Cut some petals out of the milk white crepe wrapping paper based on the pattern #28 on page 187.

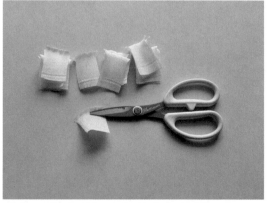

6 Scrape the tip of the petal with the back of the scissors until it bends.

7 The side view of the petals after the scraping is done.

8 Prepare several ball-headed rods of different sizes to simulate the bulging head of the lily of the valley. The ball-headed rods can also be replaced by other ball-shaped objects.

9 Wrap the petals around the head of the rod. Try hard to make it arch.

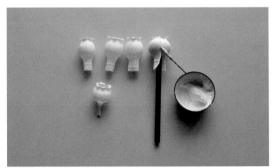

10 Pick some white latex with the tooth pick, apply it to where the petals meet, and then paste them together.

11 Press the interface tightly.

12 Make a three-dimensional flower by gathering together the bottoms of the petals by pinching.

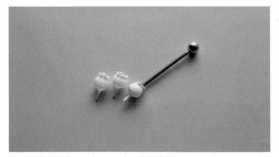

13 Sometimes, the petals might become sunken due to the pinching. When this is the case, make the sunken part bugle out with a smaller ball-headed rod.

14 Cut the redundant part at the bottom of the flower.

15 Follow the previous steps to make more flowers.

16 Apply a thick layer of white latex to the bottoms of the stamens from step 4.

17 Pass the stamen through the center of the flower and secure it at the bottom of the flower.

18 Pinch the bottom of the flower tightly. Keep rolling the bottom until it becomes round and smooth.

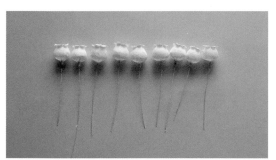

19 Some finished flowers.

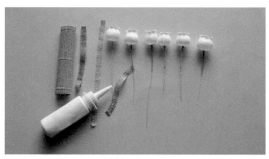

20 Cut some long strips out of the green crepe wrapping paper, pull them open, apply glue to them, and wrap them around the iron wires.

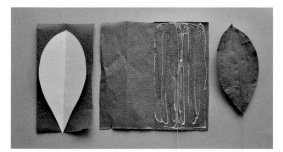

21 Cut a strip with an appropriate size out of the green crumpled paper. Apply white latex onto its right half. Place the #26 iron wire along its central line. Paste the left and right halves together so that the iron wire is securely fixed. Cut a leaf out of the paper based on the patterns #30 and #31 on page 187.

22 While the glue is drying out, use your fingernail to scrape some veins on the leaf.

23 Make three to four leaves of different sizes.

24 Cut some long strips out of the green crepe wrapping paper. Use them to wrap the buds and flowers around the #18 iron wire from small to large and from top to bottom.

25 Paste more flowers onto the #18 iron wire in appropriate density.

26 Organize the flowers. Increase or reduce the number of flowers in the way you like.

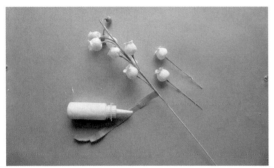

27 Arrange the leaves at the bottom of the iron wire.

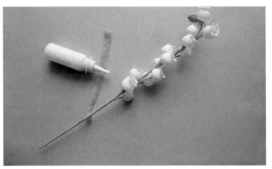

28 Cut some husks out of the brown yoshire paper based on the pattern #29 on page 187.

29 Paste several husks onto the back of the branch in good order.

30 Thus strings of lilies of the valley are complete.

8. The Corn Poppy

Corn poppies are of stunning beauty, like colorful butterflies hovering among green leaves, either simple and elegant or enthusiastic and eye-dazzling. In China, they have another name—Beauty Yu—for they are considered the incarnation of the beautiful wife of a famous general in the late Qin Dynasty (221–206 BC), Yu Ji (?–202 BC), who, seeing there was no chance for his husband to break through the besiege, killed herself to show her loyalty to their love. Later, out of her tomb there grew a lovely flower, which was named Beauty Yu in honor of this lady.

The language of the flower: loyalty to whom one loves.

Xiaoman (Grain Budding): May 20–22

Xiaoman is the 8th solar term according to the 24 terms of the year. It describes that the summer grain and corps start to plump but not yet mature. During this time, corn poppies are blooming all over China, like butterflies dancing in the late spring.

Materials and Tools

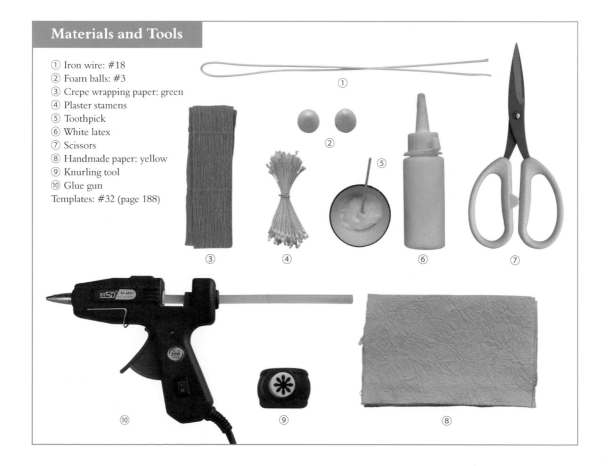

1. Iron wire: #18
2. Foam balls: #3
3. Crepe wrapping paper: green
4. Plaster stamens
5. Toothpick
6. White latex
7. Scissors
8. Handmade paper: yellow
9. Knurling tool
10. Glue gun
Templates: #32 (page 188)

How to Make It

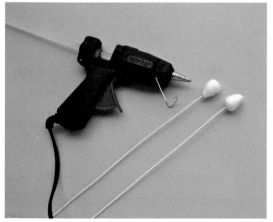

1 Fix the foam balls on the iron wires with the glue gun.

2 Draw the elastic crepe wrapping paper level and cut a round piece out of it.

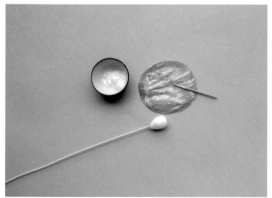

3 Apply some white latex evenly on the round paper.

4 Wrap the foam ball from step 1 with the round paper and pinch the bottom of the ball tightly together. This will serve as the flower core. Then make eight small petals out of the yellow handmade paper with the knurling tool.

5 Paste the petal on the top of the core, imitating the stamen of the corn poppy.

6 Arrange a bunch of plaster stamens side by side, and apply some white latex in the middle part. Cut the stamens in half after the white latex dries. The bottoms of the cut stamens remain gathered together.

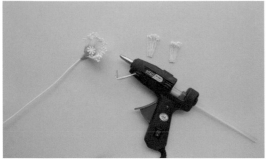

7 Fix the stamens evenly around the core with the glue gun and make them taller than the core.

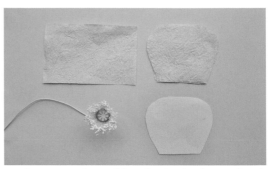

8 Cut some petals out of the yellow handmade paper based on the pattern #32 on page 188.

9 Fold the petal lengthwise with very little space in between.

10 The final effect is as shown on the left in the picture.

11 Put both ends of the petal between your fingers and twist it with force.

12 Twist it again with force in the opposite direction.

13 Unfold the petal and make it bulge out from middle with your fingers. This way, the petal looks more three-dimensional.

14 Scrape out the veins of the petal with the holder of the nicking tool.

15 Make four to eight petals following steps 8 to 14.

16 Apply some glue to the bottom of the petal.

17 Paste two petals symmetrically onto the bottom of the flower core.

18 Side effect after pasting the petals.

19 Paste two more petals in the spaces between the previous two petals.

20 Paste the last two petals in the spaces between the previous four petals.

21 A bird's-eye-view of the work after all the six petals are pasted together.

22 Cut a long and thin strip out of the green crepe wrapping paper. Draw it level, apply some glue on it, and twine it around the iron wire.

23 The iron wire should be wrapped evenly in thickness.

24 Cut smaller petal out of the leftover paper and use the petal to make flower buds. Twist it to make it soft in the same way the bigger petals are twisted and then unfold it.

25 Make some small petals of different sizes.

26 Apply some white latex to the petals and paste them around the foam ball to make a flower bud.

27 Cut some long and thin strips out of the green crepe wrapping paper. Twist each one with force in the center, and then fold it in half and cut it from the central point to form two calyxes. Make the calyxes bulge out with your finger pulp to create a three-dimensional effect.

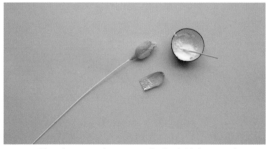

28 Glue the two calyxes onto the bud. Make sure that they vary slightly in height.

29 Apply some glue to the green crepe wrapping paper and wrap it around the iron wire.

30 You can make several flowers and buds using crepe wrapping paper of different colors, which, if well organized, can form a picture rich in color.

9. The Jasmine Flower

Just as is sung in a well-known Chinese folk song of the same name, the jasmine flower is pure white, exquisite and fragrant. Getting tired of the voluptuous beauty of other flowers, one may take an immediate liking to the simple but elegant jasmine flower. In ancient times, the flower was often worn by girls on their hairpins to show exquisite gentleness, just as a poet in the Qing Dynasty once wrote "the fragrant and jade-like jasmine flower often blooms on the hair of beauties." With some pure white jasmine flowers inside the room, one may feel mentally refreshed.

The language of the flower: geniality and simplicity.

Mangzhong (Grain in Ear): June 5–7

Mangzhong is the 9th solar term according to the 24 terms of the year, meaning crops with awns become ripe. This is also the busiest time for farmers who sow seeds for the next harvest. It is right in this period that jasmine flowers blossom. Set off by green leaves, the white flowers are indeed elegant and beautiful.

Materials and Tools

① Float-dye paper: gray-green
② Crepe wrapping paper: gray-green
③ Handmade paper: white
④ Colored pencils (grass-green)
⑤ Iron wires: #18, #24
⑥ Toothpick
⑦ Cotton thread
⑧ Needle-nose pliers
⑨ Scissors
⑩ Foam balls: #1
⑪ White latex
Templates: #33–#39 on page 188

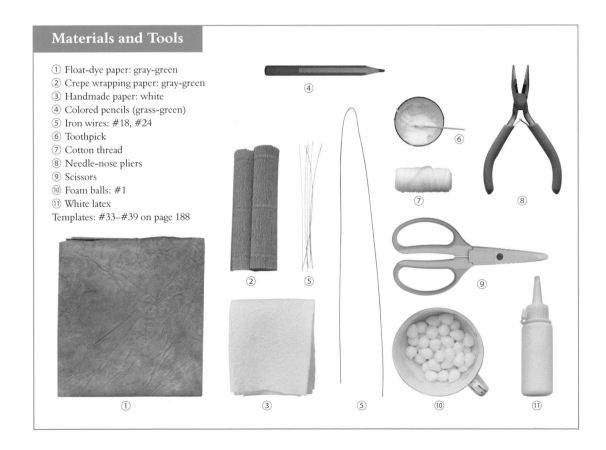

How to Make It

1 Cut some petals out of the white handmade paper based on the pattern #33 on page 188. Twist the petals into thin and long strips.

2 Keep intact one end of the strip but unfold the other end. Pass the #24 iron wire through the foam ball. Keep the ball fixed by bending the iron wire with the needle-nose pliers.

3 Now it is time to make the flower bud. Glue the petals around the foam ball with white latex until the ball is fully wrapped. Tie the bottom of the flower bud onto the iron wire with the cotton thread.

4 Apply some white latex to the top of the flower bud. Carefully glue the tips of several petals onto the flower bud. Then paste the petals onto the bud one by one from inside to outside and be sure to fasten the bottom of the flower bud with the cotton thread. This way, a bud is complete.

5 Now it is time to make full-blown flowers. First, cut some fringes out of the square gray-green crepe wrapping paper based on the pattern #36 on page 188; these will be used to make the flower core. Then, apply some white latex to one side of the fringe, wrap it around one end of the #24 iron wire, and pinch them tightly together.

6 Apply some white latex on the surface of the core and paste the petals on it.

7 A completed product should look like this one in the picture.

8 Paste enough petals around the core, pinch them tightly together, and fix them by wrapping the cotton thread around the bottom of the petals.

9 Make the petals more natural-looking by moving aside those that overlap each other.

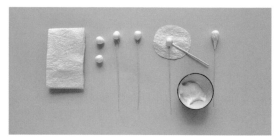

10 Pass the iron wire through the foam ball following step 2. Cut some round pieces out of the white handmade paper based on the pattern #35 on page 188. Apply some white latex on the cut paper and wrap it around the foam balls to make some small buds.

11 Cut the white handmade paper into strips, and wrap them around the bottoms of the completed flowers. Be careful to make it clean, smooth and natural-looking.

12 Paint the bottoms of the flowers with a grass-green or gray pencil.

13 Cut some calyxes out of the gray green crepe wrapping paper based on the pattern #34 on page 188. Twist the tip of the calyx and wrap it evenly around the bottom of the flower. Twine the gray-green crepe wrapping paper strips around where the calyx and the iron wire meet until it gets thicker.

14 Next, make some leaves with the gray-green float dyed paper. Apply some white latex to half of the paper, place the #24 iron wire on the side of the paper with glue on it, and fold the paper lengthwise so both sides are glued together. Cut the shape of a leaf out of the paper based on the patterns #37 to #39 on page 188 and you actually get two leaves of the same shape, which are glued together.

15 Create some deep leaf veins with your fingernail.

16 Scrape the edge of the leaf with your fingernail to make it more natural-looking.

17 Repeat the above steps to make more buds, flowers and leaves.

18 Combine two to three flowers and flower buds at random, place some leaves at the bottom of the branch in picturesque disorder, and fasten the leaves onto the branch by wrapping them with glued gray-green crepe wrapping paper.

19 A group of completed branches of flowers.

20 Twine several branches of flowers together at random with glued gray-green crepe wrapping paper.

21 Apply some glue to the gray-green crepe wrapping paper and twine it around the #18 iron wire. Also fasten some smaller branches onto the iron wire to make it steadier and longer.

22 Twine the rest of the smaller branches onto the iron wire as well.

23 Wrap the two longer iron wires together with a glued crepe wrapping paper strip to form a thicker branch. Add some bigger leaves to the branch at random.

24 Complete the whole work by bending the iron wire and adjusting the branch posture.

10. The Pomegranate Blossom

Fiery pomegranate blossoms hanging heavily on branches are a gorgeous view, especially when spring is gone and other flowers have withered. The pomegranate carries the message of "the more sons, the more blessings" and symbolizes a prosperous life in Chinese tradition. Therefore, many Chinese would plant one or two pomegranate trees in their courtyards for prosperity in life.

The language of the flower: being blessed with many offsprings.

Xiazhi (Summer Solstice): June 21–22

Xiazhi is the 10th solar term according to the 24 terms of the year, meaning the coming of the hot summer. By this time, the pomegranate blossoms have been furiously blooming, as if competing for the first to usher in the scorching summer.

Materials and Tools

① Handmade tape: brown
② Iron wires: #22, #26
③ Pliers
④ Handmade paper: green
⑤ Crumpled paper: red
⑥ Paper rattans: tangerine red, yellow
⑦ Crepe paper: red
⑧ A furcated tree branch
⑨ Scissors
⑩ White latex
⑪ Toothpick
Templates: #40–#43 (page 189)

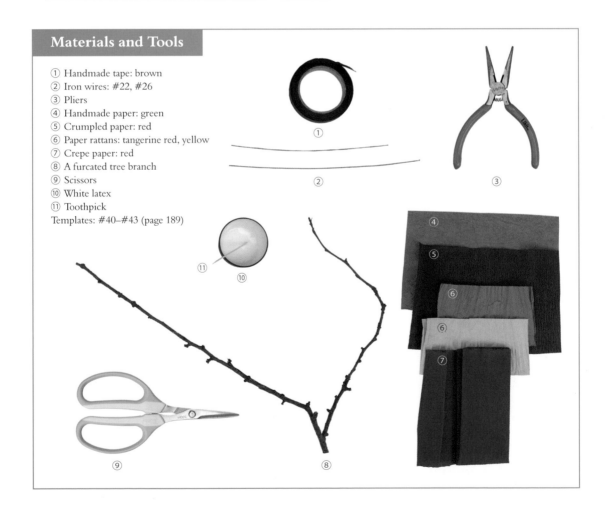

How to Make It

1 Cut a 4-by-20-centimeter strip out of the red crumpled paper.

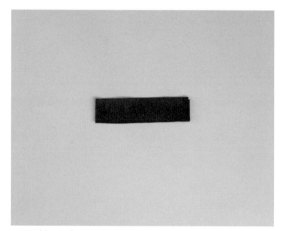

2 Pull open the elastic strip.

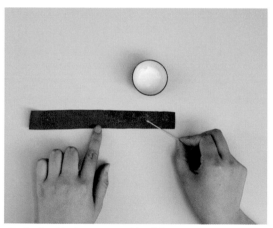

3 Apply white latex to one side of the strip.

4 Fold it to form a double-layer strip.

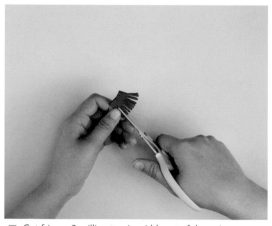

5 Cut fringes 2 millimeters in width out of the strip.

6 Rub the fringes into strands.

7 Bend one end of the #22 iron wire into a hook.

8 Hook a small section of the fringes and clamp the hook tightly with the pliers.

9 Apply white latex to the part below the fringes.

10 Wrap the strip around the hook to form the core of the flower.

11 Fold the yellow paper rattan in half several times. Cut scraps out of it as shown in the picture.

12 Apply white latex onto the top of the core.

13 Complete the core of the flower by dipping it into the scraps in imitation of pollen. Follow the above-mentioned method to make one more core.

14 Cut some petals out of the red crepe paper based on the pattern #42 on page 189.

15 Make the petals bulge out in the middle with your fingertip.

16 Apply white latex onto the bottom of the petals and arrange three to five of them into a cluster.

17 Rub the bottom of the cluster into a strand. Make more petal clusters.

18 Paste the clusters of petals in turn around the core.

19 Paste single petals onto the outermost layer.

20 A branch of the flower is complete.

21 Apply white latex onto the bottoms of three to five petal clusters. Arrange them together to form the bud.

22 The flower and the bud completed.

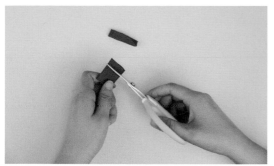

23 Cut a long strip, 0.5 centimeter in width, out of the red crepe paper.

24 Apply white latex to the strip and intertwine it around where the bottom of the bud and the iron wire meet.

25 Thicken the bottoms of the flower, bud, and another core by wrapping them with paper strips.

26 Cut a 10-by-6-centimeter rectangle out of the tangerine red paper rattan. Apply white latex to half of the rectangle and then fold it in half.

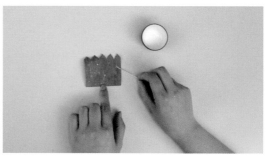

27 Divide the double-layer rectangular strip into five equal sections and then fold it as shown in the picture. Cut a pointed shape at one end. Or you can cut the shape out of the paper based on the pattern #40 on page 189.

28 Unfold the strip and apply white latex onto one side.

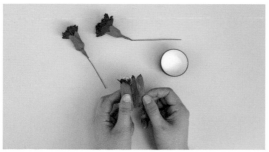

29 Wrap the strip around the flower core in step 25.

30 Cut some leaves according to the patterns #41 and #43 on page 189.

31 Apply white latex on one side of the leaf, place the #26 iron wire along its central line, and then paste another leaf of the same size onto it to form a double-layer leaf.

32 Cut the brown tape along the central line into two.

33 Arrange the leaves together with the tape.

34 Arrange the bud and leaves onto the dead tree branch from top down with the brown tape.

35 Arrange the flower and other leaves onto the branch in graceful disorder.

36 Arrange the core of the flower onto the furcated twig to complete the whole work.

11. The Hydrangea Flower

Hydrangea-growing in China can date back to the Ming and Qing dynasties more than 600 hundred years ago, when the plant was often found in gardens in southern China. Hydrangea flowers are plump and colorful and seem to extend unceasingly, looking either like a swarm of pink butterflies, or fresh and blue sea waves, or pure white clouds in the azure sky. According to Chinese mythology, the Eight Immortals were having a picnic on a mountain one day. Fascinated by the beauty of nature, He Xiangu, one of the immortals, sowed some flower seeds there. Later, the mountain was covered with eight-color flowers. For this, Hydrangea flowers are also known as Eight Immortals Flowers.

The language of the flower: bliss and reunion.

Xiaoshu (Slight Heat): July 6–8

Xiaoshu is the 11th solar term according to the 24 terms of the year. By then, the weather has become increasingly hot, which is ideal for hydrangea flowers. They bloom furiously in clusters and dance gracefully amid gentle breezes.

Materials and Tools

① Hot melt glue gun
② Iron wires: #26 (white, green)
③ Handmade tape: green
④ Handmade paper: green
⑤ Needle-nose pliers
⑥ White latex
⑦ Crepe wrapping paper: pink
Templates: #63–#65 (page 192)

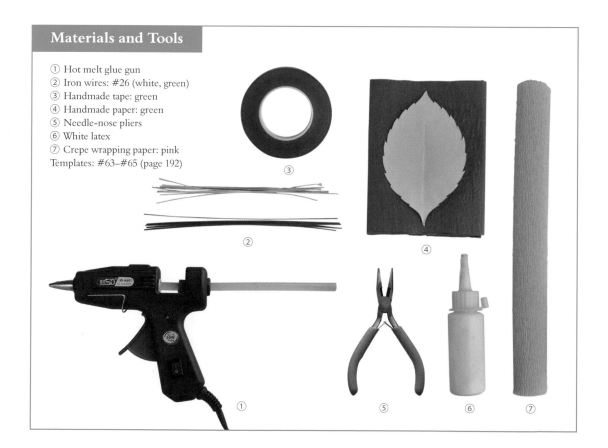

How to Make It

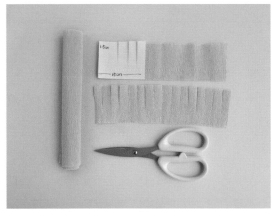

1 Cut some long strips out of the crepe wrapping paper based on the pattern #63 on page 192, which will be used to make flower petals.

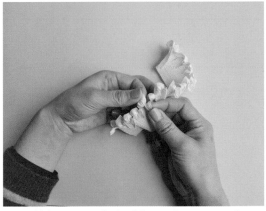

2 Hold the corner and side of the strip between your fingers and twist it into the shape of a bowknot. Treat each strip similarly.

3 Roll the petal together and pinch its bottom tightly together.

4 Fasten the bottom of the petal with the white #26 iron wire and tighten the wire with the needle-nose pliers.

5 Wrap the bottom of the petal and the iron wire tightly with the handmade green tape.

6 A contrast between the treated and untreated petals.

7 Pull out the part of the petal that curves inward to make the petal fuller.

8 Follow this method and prepare more such petals for later use.

9 Remove the surface of a green iron wire on one end with the needle-nose pliers and put it aside it for later use.

10 Wrap about six small flowers together with the green tape to make a hydrangea flower.

11 Squeeze the rest of the petals into the hydrangea flower and wrap them together tightly with the green tape. This way, the flower looks bigger and fuller.

12 Add more petals to the flower until it becomes round.

13 After the flower becomes round, fix it to the green iron wire in step 9 with the green tape.

14 Apply some glue to the bottom of the flower with the hot melt glue gun and put it aside to dry.

15 Cut two identical leaves out of the green crepe wrapping paper based on the patterns #64 and #65 on page 192, place the white iron wire in the middle of each leaf and glue them together to form a leafstalk. Make the leaf veins with your fingernail. Follow this method to make one bigger leaf and one smaller leaf.

16 After the two leaves are made, wrap them all over with the green tape.

17 Fix the two leaf stalks to the branch with green tape, one higher than the other.

18 Lastly, pull out the petals that curve inward to produce an upright and three-dimensional effect.

12. The Water Lily

The water lily, like a beauty after a bath, is a fairy in water. Supported by the large and flat lotus pad, it floats on the water surface leisurely and unfolds its tender petals gracefully. Whatever its colors—white, yellow, pink or blue— it looks pure and tranquil, as if all the earthly troubles had nothing to do with it. As the water lily "grows in mud, yet never contaminates with it; floats on waving water, yet never dances with it," it symbolizes the virtue of preserving one's own purity, simplicity, and naturalness. For this, the flower is considered the incarnation of purity and beauty in Chinese culture and is often used as offering before the Buddha.

The language of the flower: preserving one's own purity.

Dashu (Great Heat): July 22–24

Dashu is the 12th solar term of the 24 terms of the year. It is also the last solar term in summer. By this time, the hottest days in summer have already come. The water lily is in full bloom in summer, bringing people coolness and beauty.

Materials and Tools

① Green jacket tube
② Handmade paper: purple, green, yellow
③ Pliers
④ Scissors
⑤ Iron wire rods: #2 line rod, #26 iron wire
⑥ Toothpick
⑦ White latex
⑧ Handmade tape: green
Templates: #48–#52 (page 190)

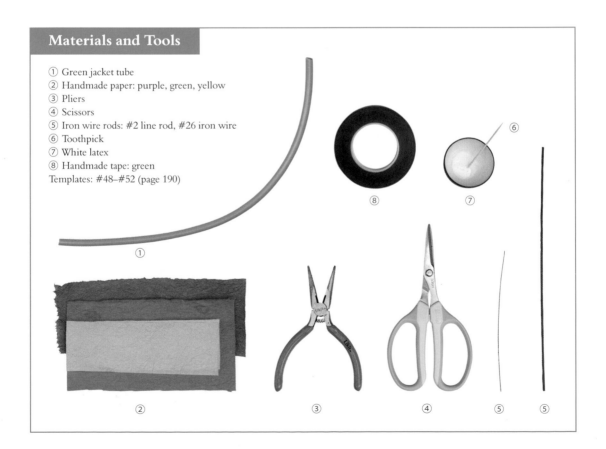

How to Make It

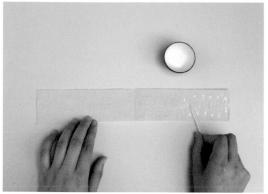

1 Cut a rectangular strip out of the yellow handmade paper. Fold it in half along the longer edge. Apply white latex onto half of the strip as shown in the picture.

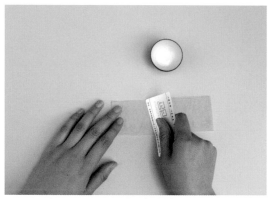

2 Paste the two parts together by folding the strip in half. Scrape the strip flat with a card.

3 Cut out grass-like fringes on one edge of the rectangular strip referring to the pattern #48 on page 190. Be careful to make the fringes dense and fine.

4 Scrape the fringes with the back of the scissors until they bend.

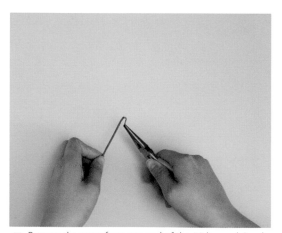

5 Remove the cover from one end of the #2 line rod. Bend this end into a hook.

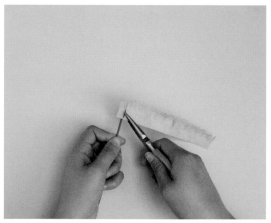

6 Hook a small part of the fringes and clamp them tightly with the pliers.

7 Apply some white latex onto the bottom of the strip.

8 Wrap the rectangular strip around the end of the iron wire. Repeat steps 1 to 4, cut a bigger rectangular strip referring to the pattern #49 on page 190, and wrap it around the smaller rectangular strip.

9 The flower core after all the wrappings is done.

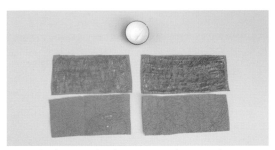

10 Apply some white latex to a purple strip and a green strip. Take out two purple strips that are as big as the previous two strips. Paste them together to form two double-layer rectangular strips.

11 Scrape the double-layer strips flat with a card and make sure that they are pasted together evenly.

12 Cut seven bigger petals and seven smaller petals out of the purple double-layer strip based on the patterns #50 and #51 on page 190.

13 Cut five to seven bigger petals out of the green-purple double-layer strip.

14 Produce a curvature on the petal by scraping it with the back of the scissors.

15 Make more such petals for later use.

16 Apply white latex onto the bottoms of the smaller petals and paste them in turn around the flower core.

17 Paste bigger petals on the second layer. The bigger petals should partly overlap with the smaller petals.

18 Paste green-purple petals on the outermost layer, with the green side facing out.

19 Insert the iron wire into the green jacket tube.

20 Wrap the jacket tube with the green tape from top to bottom and also wrap the whole line rod.

21 The flower is thus complete.

22 Cut two square strips out of the green handmade paper. Fold one of them in half twice and cut a hole in the center.

23 Take out seven #26 iron wires. Keep a section longer than half the length of the square strips, and wrap the rest part together with the green tape.

24 Pass the iron wires through the hole on the strip. Extend them towards all directions as shown in the picture. Apply some white latex onto the other green strip.

25 Paste the two green strips together.

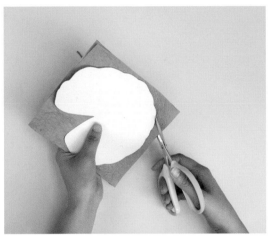

26 Cut the shape of the lily pad out of the strip based on the pattern #52 on page 190.

27 Sort out the shape of the iron wires and make the lotus pad bend naturally.

28 Scrape the edge of the lily pad with the back of the scissors until it becomes wave-like.

29 Arrange the lily pad and lily together with the green tape to produce an immaculate flower.

13. The Sunflower

Always facing the sun and resembling it in shape, the sunflower makes people feel warm and optimistic. It was introduced into China approximately in the Ming Dynasty (1368–1644), as was recorded in the work of a Ming scholar agriculturalist. The sunflower is pleasant-looking, and its nutritious and savory seeds are an indispensable snack for Chinese festivals and holidays. The whole family sitting around a table and chatting about domestic trivia over some tasty and crispy sunflower seeds is a heart-warming, happy and harmonious scene. Van Gogh, the renowned Netherland painter, was also a sunflower fan who painted a number of pictures of the flower. Under his paintbrush, the sunflowers come in various shades of yellow, mirroring the color of the sun. They are vivid and bright, showing the force of life.

The language of the flower: silent love.

Liqiu (Beginning of Autumn): August 7–9

Liqiu is the 13th solar term according to the 24 terms of the year, which means the end of summer and the beginning of autumn. The Chinese character 秋 (autumn) consists of 禾 (grain) and 火 (fire), which, put together, means the ripening of grains. This solar term is represented by the bright-looking and vigorous sunflowers.

Materials and Tools

① Handmade tape: green
② Iron wire rods: #2 line rod, #26 iron wires
③ Crepe wrapping paper: brown
④ White latex
⑤ Toothpick
⑥ Paper rattans: yellow, green
⑦ Pliers
⑧ Scissors
Templates: #69–#71 (page 193)

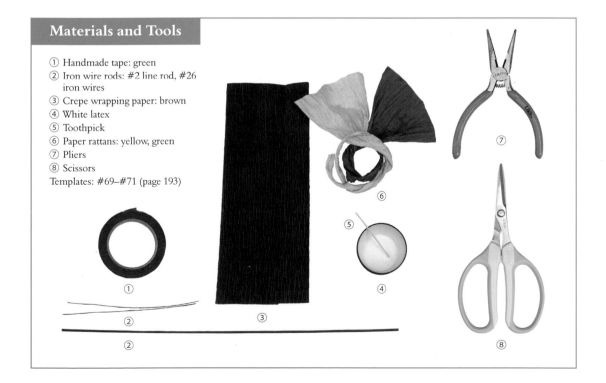

How to Make It

1 Fold the brown crepe wrapping paper in half for a couple of times and cut out of it eight long strips of 3.5 centimeters in width.

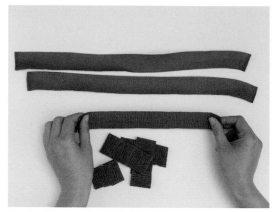

2 Gently stretch the eight strips with your hands.

3 Fold the strips in half for three times and cut fine and dense fringes on one end.

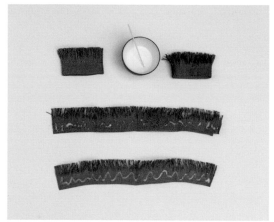

4 Apply some white latex onto the bottoms of the strips from step 3.

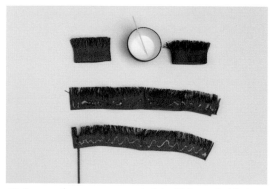

5 Remove the case on one end of the #2 line rod with the pliers, exposing the iron wire. Bend the exposed iron wire into a hook with the pliers, hook one end of the strip with it, and compress the hook with the pliers to prevent the strip from dropping off.

6 Wrap the strip tightly around the hook.

7 A flower disc is formed after wrapping.

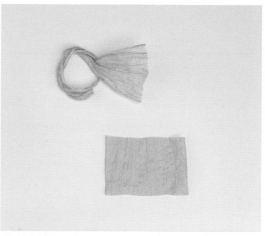

8 Unfold the yellow paper rattan and cut out of it a piece of paper 6 centimeters in length.

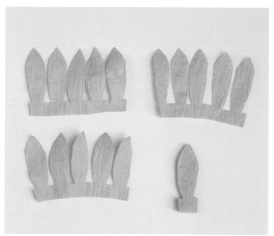

9 Cut of the paper some sunflower petals based on the pattern #69 on page 193. Make four groups of petals

10 Create a three-dimensional effect by pasting both ends of the petal bottom.

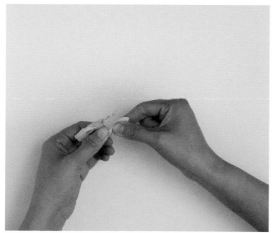

11 Twist the top of the petal to form some flower veins and then unfold it.

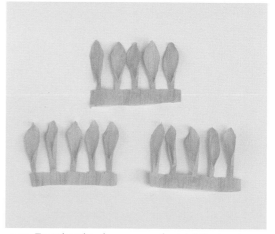

12 Treat the other three groups of petals following steps 12 and 13.

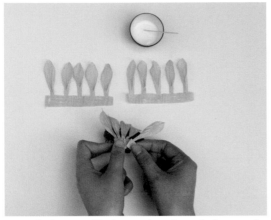

13 Apply some white latex to the strips at the bottom of the petals and paste them around the flower disc one after the other; the strips should overlap each other slightly.

14 The front view of the flower disc after all the petals are pasted on it.

15 Stretch the green paper rattan, fold it from left to right for four times to form five equal parts, and cut out of it the shape of the calyx based on the pattern #71 on page 193.

16 Unfold the calyx. Repeat the process to make a second calyx.

17 Apply some white latex on one side of the calyx and wrap it around the bottom of the flower disc. Cover the bottom of the flower disc with the two interwoven calyxes and tighten the bottoms of the calyxes by twisting them.

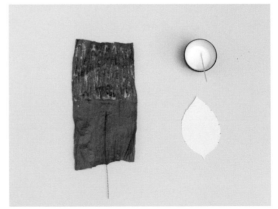

18 Extend the 15-centimeter piece of green paper rattan. Apply some white latex to its upper half, place a #26 iron wire in the middle of the lower half, and fold the paper from top to bottom so that the two parts are pasted together.

19 Cut a leaf out of the paper based on the pattern #70 on page 193. Then repeat step 20 to 21 to make one more leaf.

20 Line out the veins of the leaves with your fingernail.

21 Take a section of the green tape and cut it into two long strips.

22 Wrap the bottom of the leaf with the tape to make the leaf stalk.

23 Wrap the line rod with the green tape from the bottom of the calyx downward. Add two leaves onto the line rod in picturesque disorder.

24 Thus is completed a vigorous-looking sunflower.

14. The Cotton Rose

The cotton rose is magic in that it changes color three times a day—milk white or pink in early morning, deep red afterward, and then violet red at dusk—increasing in beauty as the day passes. In a poem, Wang Anshi (1021–1086), a well-known ancient Chinese poet, compared the cotton rose in early morning to a beauty, who, though still wearing a drowsy look, is naturally refreshing.

The language of the flower: chastity.

Chushu (Limit of Heat): August 22–24

Chushu is the 14th solar term according to the 24 terms of the year, meaning that the summer heat is gradually decreasing and the weather is turning cooler. This is the time when cotton rose is in bloom.

Materials and Tools

① Toothpick
② Plaster stamens: yellow
③ Foam balls: #2
④ White latex
⑤ Crumpled paper: green
⑥ Crepe wrapping paper: deep pink, light pink, green
⑦ Iron wires: #26, #18
⑧ Pliers
⑨ Scissors
Templates: #72–#79
(page 194)

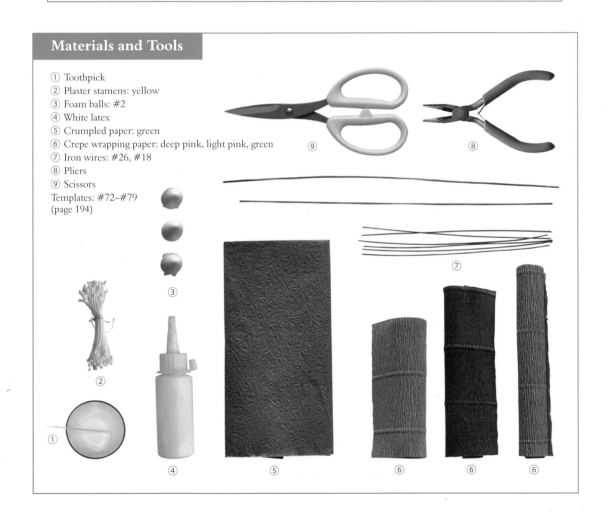

How to Make It

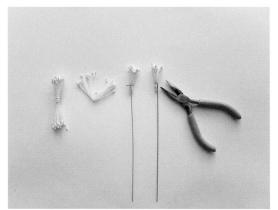

1 Take out ten plaster stamens and fold them in half. Secure them onto the #26 iron wire with the pliers.

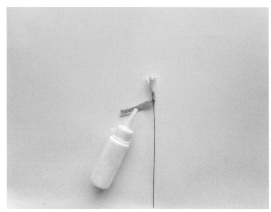

2 Cut some long strips out of the light pink crepe wrapping paper and wrap them around the iron wire at the bottom of the stamen.

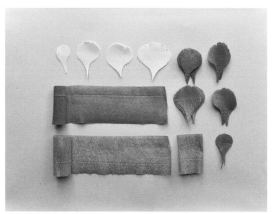

3 Cut some petals of different shades and sizes out of the pink crepe wrapping paper based on the patterns #72 to #74 on page 194.

4 A bird's-eye view of the petals.

5 Twist the petals into braids.

6 Unfold the petals. Use your fingers to make the petal edge wave-like. Scrape the petal edge with your fingernail until it turns up in a way that looks like a real flower petal.

7 Completed petals of different shapes.

8 Take four or five smallest petals of different color shades, apply white latex onto their bottoms, and paste them around the stamen.

9 Arrange the petals flexibly and avoid being too orderly.

10 Pick out petals of the same size from among the rest of the petals, excluding the biggest petals, apply white latex onto the bottoms of these petals, and pinch them into a tuftlet.

11 Arrange the biggest petals in pairs, one deep-colored and the other light-colored, and paste them together at the edges.

12 In this picture, from top to bottom, in the first row are tuftlets of petals completed in step 10, in the second row are petals in pairs completed in step 11, and in the third row are four to five big petals. The next thing to do is to arrange these petals together.

13 Apply glue onto the bottom of a tuftlet in the first row and paste it onto the flower from step 8.

14 Paste more tuftlets onto the flower and gather the whole work together at the bottom. This picture shows the bottom of the flower after four or five tuftlets are pasted onto it.

15 The flower must look full and plump from above.

16 Apply glue to the big petals in pairs and paste them into the gaps between petals.

17 Paste the big single petals into the gaps between petals as you see fit.

18 This is what a cotton rose looks like after all the pasting is done.

19 During pasting, make sure that you have applied enough white latex onto the bottom of flowers and each of the petals has been firmly secured onto the flower.

20 Pass the #26 iron wire through the #2 foam ball bud and clamp them with the pliers.

21 Cut out some small petals based on the pattern in the appendix, and paste them onto the surface of the foam ball to make a small bud.

22 Pull out the elastic green crepe wrapping paper and cut some calyxes out of it based on the pattern #75 on page 194. Apply white latex onto them and paste them evenly onto the bud. Pinch the bottom of the bud tightly.

23 Cut some supplementary calyxes based on the pattern #76 on page 194 and paste them evenly onto the bottom of the bud.

24 Follow the same method and paste the calyxes from steps 22 and 23 onto the bottom of the flower from step 19.

25 Cut pieces of paper out of the green crumbled paper based on the patterns #77 to #79 on page 194. Apply some white latex onto the right half the paper. Place a #26 iron wire along its central line, and secure it by folding the paper in half from left to right. Cut a leaf out of this paper.

26 Scrape the leaf with your fingernail to make some leaf veins.

27 Cut some long strips out of the green crepe wrapping paper, apply white latex onto them, and wrap them around the iron wires attached to the leaves, flowers and buds.

28 Wrap the leaves, buds and flowers hierarchically onto the #18 iron wire.

29 Cut some long strips out of the green crepe wrapping paper, apply white latex to them and then wrap them around the #18 iron wire.

30 Thus a plump-looking cotton rose is complete.

15. The Sword Lily

The sword lily is extremely rich in color. The red ones are regal and dignified, the pink ones enchantingly beautiful, the white ones simple but elegant, the purple ones charmingly romantic, the yellow ones noble and graceful, the orange ones gentle and restrained, the violet ones quietly elegant, the blue ones dignified and sedate, the grey ones old-fashioned but classical, and the mixed-color ones vivid and dynamic. As the forerunner of flower arrangement in the East, China has led the discussion on the methods of flower arrangement from a very early time. As early as 1599, in his *History of Vases*, Yuan Hongdao explained very clearly the artistic beauty of flower arrangement. According to him, "The flowers can neither be arranged too crowdedly nor too sparsely. The kinds of flowers used in flower arrangement should not exceed two or three, which should be arranged in picturesque disorder." What he said is exactly right for the arrangement of sword lilies, which, arranged in either direction, display unique charms, elevating the art of flower arrangement from natural beauty to artistic beauty.

The language of the flower: extraordinary-looking.

Bailu (White Dew): September 7–9

Bailu is the 15th solar term according to the 24 terms of the year. By then, the weather has turned cooler gradually and one can often find in early morning much dew on the ground and leaf surfaces, and hence the name of White Dew. This is the time when the sword lily is in full blossom.

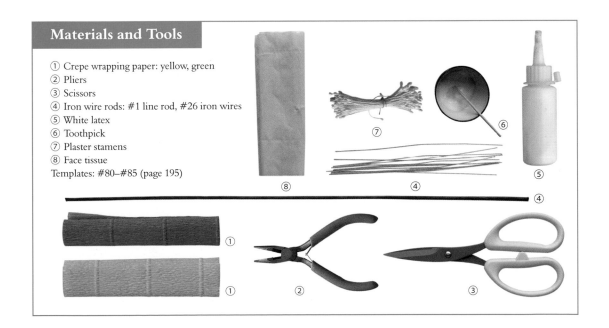

Materials and Tools

① Crepe wrapping paper: yellow, green
② Pliers
③ Scissors
④ Iron wire rods: #1 line rod, #26 iron wires
⑤ White latex
⑥ Toothpick
⑦ Plaster stamens
⑧ Face tissue
Templates: #80–#85 (page 195)

How to Make It

1 Cut three bigger petals and three smaller petals based on the patterns #80 and #81 on page 195.

2 Apply some white latex onto the middle and lower parts of the petals.

3 Paste two petals of the same size together.

4 Press them with your thumbs and dry them up.

5 Paste the three bigger petals and three smaller petals together respectively.

6 Apply some glue to the edges of the two petals on both sides and enclose the three petals as shown in the picture.

7 Press the edges tightly together.

8 This is the final effect of two groups of petals.

9 Take out four plaster stamens and fold them in half. Wrap the stamens onto the #26 iron wire with the long strips cut out of the green crepe wrapping paper. Make sure the end of the iron wire is not wrapped in.

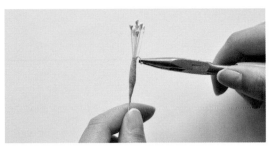

10 Bend the iron wire at the top into a hook with the pliers. Hook the green crepe wrapping paper to prevent the stamens from falling off.

11 Hide the hook by wrapping it up with the green crepe wrapping paper. Thus a complete group of stamen is made.

12 Scrape the petal with the back of the scissors until it bends naturally.

13 Use your hand to make the edge of the petal into fine waves.

14 Apply more white latex to the base of the stamen.

15 Cover the smaller petals onto the base of the stamen and pinch them tightly together.

16 Apply some white latex to the bottom of the smaller petals and arrange the bigger petals at the bottom of the smaller petals.

17 Arrange the two layers of petals as shown in the picture.

18 Pull out the elastic green crepe wrapping paper and cut the shape of a calyx out of it based on the patterns #82 and #83 on page 195.

19 Apply some white latex to the calyxes.

20 Paste the calyxes onto the flower.

21 Cut the face tissue into long strips, apply white latex to them, and wrap them around one end of the iron wire until it becomes olive-shaped. They will be used to make flower buds.

22 Paste the yellow petals and green calyxes onto the surface of the face tissue. Make some buds or half-blossoming flowers according to your own design.

23 Cut some leaves out of the green crepe wrapping paper based on the patterns #84 and #85 on page 195. Apply some white latex onto their bottoms and arrange them together in twos and threes. Scrape the tips of the leaves with the back of the scissors until they bend naturally.

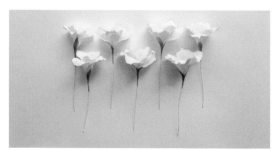

24 Follow the above method to make flowers and buds of different sizes, which will be arranged together later on.

25 Apply some white latex to the long strip cut out of the green crepe wrapping paper. Wrap the calyxes face-to-face onto one end of the #1 line rod with it.

26 Arrange the buds onto the line rod from top to bottom and from small to big.

27 Wrap the flowers in appropriate distance onto the line rod.

28 The flowers face the same direction.

29 Apply some white latex to the calyx and paste it on where the back of the flower meets with the line rod.

30 Apply some white latex to the bottom of the leaves.

31 Wrap the leaves around the line rod, one taller and the other shorter.

32 Wrap the bottom evenly with the crepe wrapping paper strips.

33 A branch of bright-colored sword lilies is complete.

16. The Dahlia

With layers upon layers of petals, the dahlia in full blossom looks like a little princess in a ballet skirt, dancing in swirls among clusters of flowers, noble and lovely. Against the rustling western wind in autumn, the dahlia displays its beauty to the fullest.

The language of the flower: auspiciousness.

Qiufen (Autumnal Equinox): September 23–24

Qiufen is the 16th solar term according to the 24 terms of the year, meaning the middle of autumn. By then, the sky is clear, the air is crisp, and everywhere you look is golden yellow. The autumn is already half gone and a chill begins to linger in the morning air. After *qiufen*, the weather turns increasingly cooler. It is during this time that dahlias are blooming magnificently in diverse colors.

Materials and Tools

① Crepe wrapping paper: green
② Handmade paper: green
③ Float-dye paper: blue
④ Foam ball: #2
⑤ Glue gun
⑥ Scissors
⑦ White latex
⑧ Iron wire rods: #1 line rod, #26 iron wires
⑨ Dotting pen
⑩ Toothpick
Templates: #53–#62
(page 191)

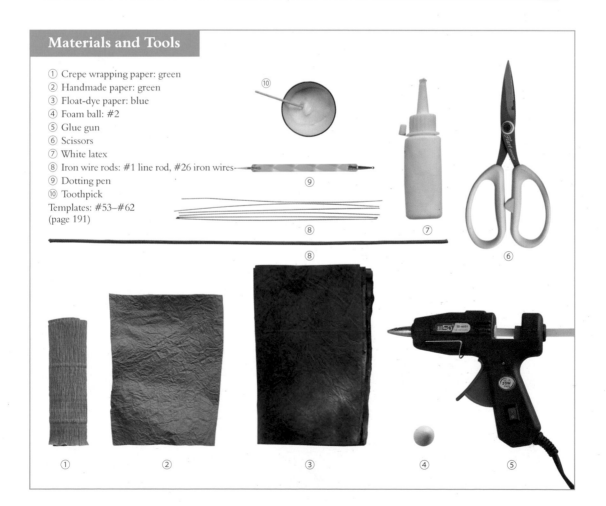

How to Make It

1 Cut a rectangular strip, about 15 centimeters long, out of the blue float-dye paper based on the size of the pattern #53 on page 191. Fold the strip from top to bottom and then unfold it. Apply white latex onto its lower half and then fold it from top to bottom again so both parts are glued together. Press it until it becomes flat and even. Cut the shape of a small inner petal based on the pattern as shown in the picture.

2 Scrape some grooves and curvatures on the petal with the dotting pen when the petal is half dry. Make the petal bend naturally.

3 A petal bending inwardly.

4 Make another small inner petal and scrape with the dotting pen some grooves and curvatures in the opposite direction on its top.

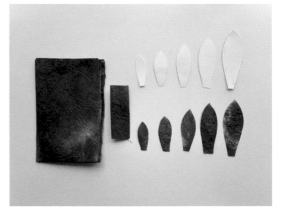

5 Put the two small inner petals aside for later use.

6 Cut several rectangular strips based on the sizes of the patterns #54 to #58 on page 191 and then make outer petals of different sizes following the patterns.

7 Finished outer petals of different sizes.

8 Twist all the petals into braids.

9 Pull the petal in opposite directions with both hands while twisting it.

10 After unfolding the petal, scrape some strip-like veins on it with your fingernail and at the same time twist the tip of the petal.

11 Fold both sides of the petal's bottom towards the middle line and press it with your hand until it becomes flat.

12 Make some more petals and categorize them according to their sizes for later use.

13 Use the glue gun to secure the foam ball onto the #1 line rod as the flower core.

14 Apply white latex onto the inner petal and wrap it around the flower core.

15 Apply some white latex to the tip of the petal, gather it and then paste it onto the foam ball. Be careful not to reveal the white foam ball. Pinch the bottom of the petal tightly together.

16 Apply some white latex to the second inner petal with its tip bending outwards and wrap it around the flower core.

17 Pinch the bottom of the flower core tightly together in the shape of an upside-down cone.

18 The top of the flower after the two inner petals are pasted.

19 Next, paste the outer petals from inside out and from small to big, one next to the other.

20 The top of the outer petals.

21 After a layer of outer petals is pasted, apply white latex onto the bottom of the petals. Paste another layer of petals on it, each petal filling the gap between previous petals.

22 The top of the flower after two layers of petals are pasted.

23 Make sure that the next layer of outer petals is a bit higher than the previous one.

24 The top of the flower after several layers of petals are pasted.

25 The outer the petals, the more white latex should be used, so that the petals are firmly glued together.

26 Start to paste bigger petals. Pay attention to the overall look of the flower. The petals should be arranged evenly. Wherever there is a gap, paste more petals to make it fuller.

27 This is how the back of the flower looks. It should be clean, full and in good order.

28 The top of the flower also looks full and plump.

29 After all the petals are pasted, apply white latex onto the bottom of the flower for the pasting of calyx.

30 Pull the elastic green crepe wrapping paper open and cut a piece of round paper out of it based on the pattern #59 on page 191. Fold it in half several times, cut out some indentions on it and a hole in its center, and then unfold it. This will serve as the calyx.

31 Pass the line rod through the hole in the calyx and paste the calyx evenly onto the bottom of the flower. Make a similar calyx and paste it outside the first calyx. The two calyxes will be able to prop up the flower from the bottom firmly.

32 The bottom of the flower with two layers of calyxes.

33 Cut a rectangular strip of an appropriate size out of the green handmade paper based on the leaf pattern #60 on page 191. Apply some white latex to the iron wire and paste it firmly in the middle of the strip. Cut a leaf out of the strip and scrape some veins on it. Cut a long strip out of the crepe wrapping paper and wrap it around the leaf stalk. Follow this method to make more leaves of assorted sizes.

34 Cut another strip out of the green crepe wrapping paper, apply some white latex to it, and wrap it around the line rod to make it thicker. Organize the leaves in picturesque disorder onto the line rod.

35 Make another inner petal and a flower core, apply some white latex to it, and paste it around the flower core as the bud.

36 Pinch the bottom of the bud tightly together.

37 The top of the bud.

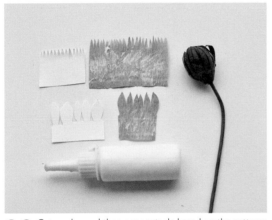

38 Cut a calyx and then a receptacle based on the patterns #61 and #62 on page 191. Apply some white latex onto them so they can be pasted onto the bud. Be careful not to apply white latex on the saw tooth of the calyx and the receptacle.

39 Paste the calyx at the bottom of the bud and the receptacle outside the calyx.

40 This is the completed bud. Bend the receptacle outwards with your hands.

41 Arrange the leaves onto the bud to finish the dahlia.

17. The Green Chrysanthemum

The chrysanthemum, as one of the four gentlemen flowers, has garnered much praise from men of letters in the time-honored history of China. It is particularly known for its noble-mindedness and the spirit of blooming against cold and snow. The household poetic lines "While picking chrysanthemums beneath the eastern fence, my gaze upon the southern mountain rests" offer a vivid depiction of the carefree attitude and elegant taste of the poet who was away from the madding crowd. They also set off the elegance and self-pride of the flower perfectly. In China, the chrysanthemum is in full bloom during the Double Ninth Festival (Sept. 9) and it has become a tradition for people to appreciate chrysanthemums over a cup of wine.

   The language of the flower: pure and noble-minded.

Hanlu (Cold Dew): October 8–9

Hanlu is the 17th solar term according to the 24 terms of the year. By then, the dew is going to freeze due to the cold, and hence the name of Cold Dew. After this period, the weather turns dry and the day is hot while the night is cool. It is the right time to appreciate chrysanthemums, which come in various colors and vie with each other for most glamorous.

Materials and Tools

① Float-dye paper: green
② Crepe wrapping paper: deep green, medium green, light green
③ Toothpick
④ Glue gun
⑤ Iron wire rods: #24 iron wires, #1 line rod
⑥ Scissors
⑦ White latex
⑧ Dotting pen
Templates: #92–#97 (page 197), #98–#100 (page 198)

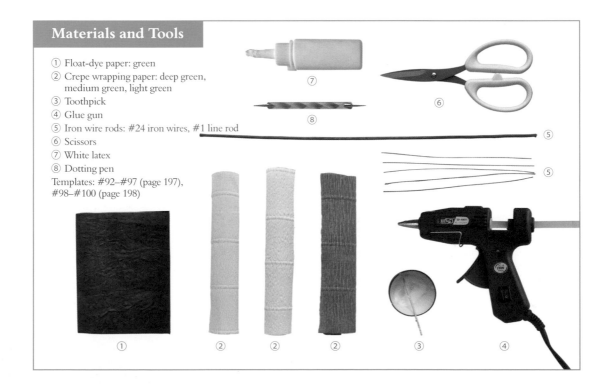

How to Make It

1 Fold the rectangular medium green crepe wrapping paper (about 30 centimeters in length) in half several times. Cut the shape of a chrysanthemum core out of it based on the pattern #92 on page 197, the top of which is fringe-shaped. Apply white latex to the petal and then wrap it around one end of the line rod and cut the fringes on the top even finer to serve as the flower core.

2 Fold the paper with a total length of about 50 centimeters referring to step 1. Cut the shape of a medium green petal based on the pattern #93 on page 197. Apply white latex to it and twist its top into braids. Twist with force to prevent it from loosening.

3 This is how the top of the petal is twisted.

4 Scrape the braids with the tip of the dotting pen and make them bend naturally. This will be used as the inner petal.

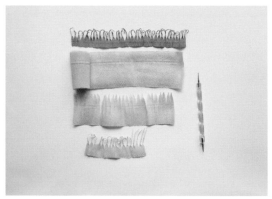

5 Next, cut the second layer of petal out of the light green crepe wrapping paper, which is 1 centimeter taller than the inner petal. Twist the top into braids and then scrape them until they bend naturally.

6 Apply white latex onto the first inner petal and wrap it around the flower core. Pinch it tightly together. The length of the petal depends on the flower size you wish to make.

7 After the wrapping is done, scrape the tip of the petal that does not bend with the tip of the dotting pen.

8 Apply white latex to the second layer of light green petal and wrap it around the medium green petal.

9 This is how it looks after the two petals are wrapped.

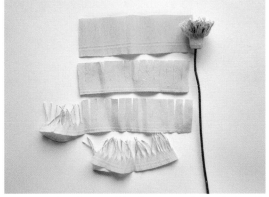

10 Based on the size of the flower core, choose the length of the strip to be cut out of the medium-green and light-green crepe wrapping paper for the making of the outer petal, which should be slightly taller than the inner petals. Cut the shape of the petal based on the pattern #94 on page 197. The fringes can be made finer to mimic those of real chrysanthemums.

11 Fold the medium green and light green crepe wrapping paper in half several times. Cut the shapes of petals out of it with a progressive increase in height referring to the patterns #96 and #97 on page 197, which will serve as outer petals.

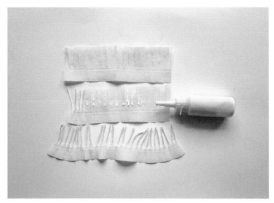

12 Apply white latex to the fringes of the petal and twist the fringes into braids.

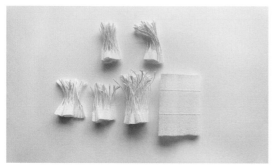

13 Categorize the twisted petals according to their sizes. Make more petals in each category for later use.

14 You can arrange the petals from short to tall for ease of use.

15 Apply white latex to the outer petals from short to tall and wrap them evenly around the inner petals.

16 While wrapping, keep the bottom of the petal neat.

17 This is how it looks like after the petals are wrapped. Sort out the fringes with your hands.

18 A bird's-eye-view of the flower.

19 Next, wrap the biggest light green petal as the outermost layer.

20 The top of the flower after all the wrappings are done.

21 The back of the flower after all the wrappings are done.

22 Secure the round disc at the bottom with the glue gun so that it is firmly fixed on the flower core. The head of the flower is complete.

23 Cut a long strip out of the deep green crepe wrapping paper. The length of the strip should be bigger than the girth of the flower head. Pull the elastic strip open, fold it and cut the shape of the indented calyx out of it based on the pattern #95 on page 197.

24 Scrape the indentions on the calyx with the back of the scissors until they bend.

25 Apply some white latex to the part of the calyx other than the indentions and wrap it around the bottom of the flower head.

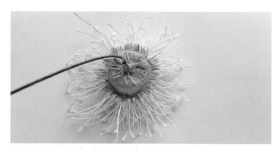

26 Tighten the bottom of the calyx inward before the white latex dries.

27 Make another calyx and paste it outside the first calyx, but in a slightly lower position. This way, the bottom of the flower looks more natural.

28 Cut the crepe wrapping paper into long strips, apply white latex to them and wrap them evenly around the line rod.

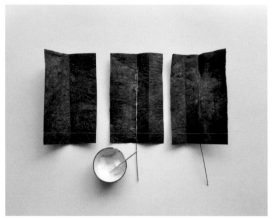

29 Make single-layer leaves with the green float-dye paper. Take some white latex with the toothpick and apply it onto the #24 iron wire. Place the iron wire in the center of the rectangular strip, fold the strip and press it tightly against the iron wire, and unfold the strip after the glue dries up.

30 Cut three leaves, one big, one medium and one small, based on the patterns #98 to #100 on page 198.

31 Scrape veins on the leaf with your fingernail. Keep scraping the leaf until it bends naturally.

32 Apply white latex onto the deep green crepe wrapping paper strip and wrap it around the leaf stalk.

33 Apply white latex onto the deep green crepe wrapping paper strip and use it to secure the leaves onto the line rod from top to bottom and from small to big.

34 This is the work after the leaves are added.

35 Pull aside the outer petals to reveal the inner petals. Soften the outer petals and make them easier to roll by applying some white latex onto them.

36 Use your hand to curl the outer petals inward with the help of the dotting pen.

37 Put some white latex on your fingers and continue to curl the petals inward.

38 Curl the petals in the peripheral area inward with the tip of the dotting pen.

39 The curling part of the petals can be different in length.

40 This is the flower after all the curling is done.

41 This is the back of the flower.

42 A green chrysanthemum in full blossom is thus complete.

18. The Red Spider Lily

The red spider lily is fiery red, with its petals extending in all directions, as if embracing the days of passion and spirit, or dashing ahead toward the passionate love. The flower is unique: when it blooms, there are no leaves; when the leaves are green, the flower is yet to bloom. In other words, the leaves and the flower never meet each other. This strong contrast adds another stirring temperament to this fiery flower. In Buddhism, the red spider lily is a flower in paradise and those who see it will have their sins removed automatically. The flower also inspires people to forget unhappy things from the past and keep away from old troubles.

The language of the flower: love you dearly.

Shuangjiang (Frost's Descent): October 23–24

Shuangjiang is the 18th solar term according to the 24 terms of the year. By then, the weather turns cold gradually and frost begins to descend. It is the last solar term in autumn and therefore also means the beginning of winter. As one of the four auspicious flowers, the red spider lily adds luster to this season.

Materials and Tools

① Green jacket tube
② Iron wire rods: #2 line rod, #22 and #26 iron wires
③ Handmade tape: red, green
④ Crepe wrapping paper: red
⑤ Pliers
⑥ Scissors
⑦ Toothpick
⑧ White latex
Template: #13 (page 184)

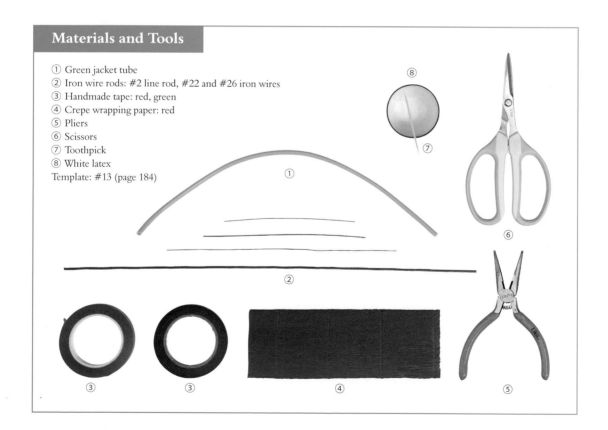

How to Make It

1 Cut thirty-six petals out of the red crepe wrapping paper based on the pattern #13 on page 184.

2 Apply white latex onto a 10 centimeter length of #26 iron wire.

3 Place the iron wire along the central line of the petal.

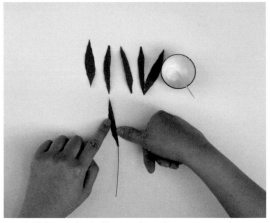

4 Fold the petal in half, press along the iron wire with your thumb until it is firmly secured to the petal.

5 Unfold the petal when the white latex dries up. Use your fingers to make the edge of the petal wavy.

6 Make six groups of petals following the above methods.

7 Take out a section of red tape and cut it in half along the central line.

8 Take out three 20-centimeter pieces of #26 iron wire and wrap them with the red tape to mimic the stamens.

9 Fold the three stamens in half. Hook them at the center with a #22 iron wire. Clamp the hook and stamens with the pliers.

10 Wrap the linking part between the iron and stamens with the red tape.

11 Arrange six petals one after another around the stamens.

12 Wrap the bottom of the petals tightly with the green tape.

13 Turn the petals inside out.

14 Sort out the stamens with your hand, making it slightly S-shaped.

15 Make six identical flowers.

16 Arrange the flowers one after another onto the #2 line rod.

17 Fix the flowers onto the line rod by wrapping them together with the green tape.

18 Insert the thinner end of the line rod into the green jacket tube and wrap the tube with the green tape until it becomes thicker.

19 Thus a unique red spider lily is complete.

19. The Maple Leaf

In autumn, the maple leaves turn from green to yellow and then to red, covering every street with a red carpet and forming a unique autumn scene. Falling gracefully from the branches, the palm-shaped leaves bring fiery enthusiasm and vitality to autumn. Like warm sunshine in the cool autumn sky, they also remind you of the good old days.

Chinese people have long recognized the value of maple leaves for appreciation. For instance, the poetic lines "I stopped the carriage to appreciate the maple leaves in the sunset. The leaves covered with frost were redder than the blooming flowers in February" by the Tang poet Du Mu (803–853) describe the pretty scenery of maple leaves in the dusk, and "I see a thousand hills crimsoned through by their serried woods deep-dyed" by Mao Zedong (1893–1976) creates a bold and heroic atmosphere.

The language of the maple leaf: fortitude.

Lidong (Beginning of Winter): November 7–8

Lidong is the 19th solar term according to the 24 terms of the year, meaning the beginning of winter. The reddening maple leaves bid a final farewell to autumn.

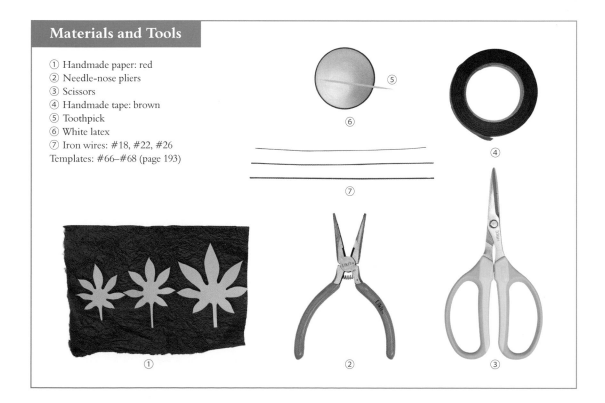

Materials and Tools

① Handmade paper: red
② Needle-nose pliers
③ Scissors
④ Handmade tape: brown
⑤ Toothpick
⑥ White latex
⑦ Iron wires: #18, #22, #26
Templates: #66–#68 (page 193)

How to Make It

1 Fold the red handmade paper in half. Cut the three sizes of leaves out of the red paper based on the patterns #66 to #68 on page 193, two for each pattern.

2 Apply some white latex on one side of the leaf and paste the #26 iron wire onto its middle.

3 Paste the two leaves of the same size exactly together.

4 Cut some indentions on the edge of the leaf, in imitation of the maple leaf's natural shape.

5 Prepare more leaves of different sizes.

6 Cut some strips of about 0.5 centimeter in width out of the red handmade paper.

7 Apply some white latex to one side of the strip and wrap it around the iron wire at the bottom of the leaf.

8 Take a section from the brown tape and cut it along the central line.

9 Wrap the maple leaves from small to big and from top to bottom onto the #22 iron wire with the cut tape.

10 Prepare several groups of maple leaves by repeating steps 7 to 10.

11 Wrap some twigs onto the #18 iron wire with the brown tape.

12 Thus big branches of maple leaves are complete.

20. The Sacred Bamboo

The sacred bamboo is graceful and beautiful. It is emerald green, with durable red fruits hanging heavily from the branches. The best seasons to appreciate the sacred bamboo are autumn and winter when its leaves are turning red. In traditional Chinese flower arrangement, the sacred bamboo is often arranged together with full-blown winter-sweets and pine branches to symbolize the great vitality of life, as all of them are frost-resisting plants. Again, for this reason, they have often appeared under the pen of men of letters to symbolize noble characters. Against the desolate winter, the red leaves and fruits of the sacred bamboo are extremely eye-catching. The berries, like agates, hang heavily from the branches, giving people a sense of joy and happiness.

The language of the sacred bamboo: health and longevity.

Xiaoxue (Lesser Snow): November 22–23

Xiaoxue is the 20th solar term according to the 24 terms of the year. By then, the temperature has kept dropping, but warm days still appear when it is clear and still. During this period, the graceful sacred bamboo has borne strings of red fruits, which are beautiful in the desolate winter, especially when a heavy snow falls.

Materials and Tools

① Handmade paper: green
② Crepe wrapping paper: green
③ White latex
④ Pliers
⑤ Scissors
⑥ Toothpick
⑦ Chalks
⑧ Artificial berries
⑨ Iron wires: #26
Templates: #101–#103
(page 199)

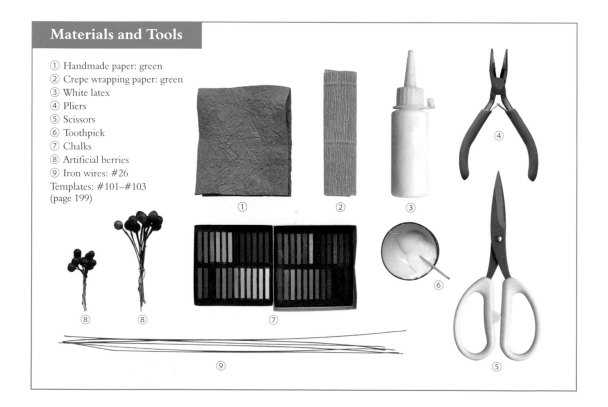

How to Make It

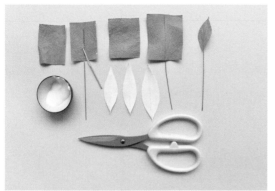

1 Cut some rectangular strips out of the green handmade paper based on the sizes of the patterns #101 to #103 on page 199. Apply some white latex onto the iron wires and place them in the middle of the strips. Fold the strips in half and press them hard so that the iron wires and the strips are firmly pasted together. Unfold the strips after the white latex dries up. Cut the patterns of leaves out of the strips. Make more leaves of various sizes.

2 Cut some long strips out of the green crepe wrapping paper, apply some white latex onto them, and wrap the leaf stalks of various sizes together.

3 Arrange all these leaves into one big branch. Secure them with glued crepe wrapping paper strips.

4 Follow steps 1 to 3 to make several branches of the sacred bamboo.

5 Now let's dye the leaves. First, scrape the iron-oxide-red chalk for some powder.

6 Pick up some powder with a strip of the crepe wrapping paper and dab it on the leaves evenly. Don't let the powder gather at one point.

7 Dab some powder on each leaf.

8 Unfasten the bunch of artificial berries and straighten the bent iron wires on them with your hands.

9 Apply some white latex onto the long strip cut out of the green crepe wrapping paper and wrap the berries together with it from top to bottom and from yellow to deep red.

10 Make three groups of berries as shown in the picture. One of them with more berries on it serves as the main branch. Add three more #26 iron wires to the main branch to make it thicker and longer by wrapping it with the green crepe wrapping paper.

11 If the main branch is too soft, add two more #26 iron wires and wrap it with the green crepe wrapping paper.

12 Thicken the main branch by wrapping it with the green crepe wrapping paper and add one group of leaves onto it.

13 Arrange all groups of leaves onto the main branch. Wrap the branch until it becomes even in thickness. Thus a branch of scared bamboo with green leaves and red fruits is complete.

21. The Camellia

The camellia boasts various species. Plump-looking and elegant, it is a traditional ornamental flower and one of the 10 most famous flowers in China. For its strength of character and beauty, it has won praises from men of letters both in the past and at present. The flower gained the greatest fame in the Tang Dynasty and Song Dynasty.

The language of the flower: forbearance and modesty.

Daxue (Great Snow): December 6–8

Daxue is the 21st solar term according to the 24 terms of the year, meaning the coming of heavy snow. The camellia is also known as a winter-resistant flower, blooming in full vitality against the snow, resembling the forbearance and modesty of women in the East.

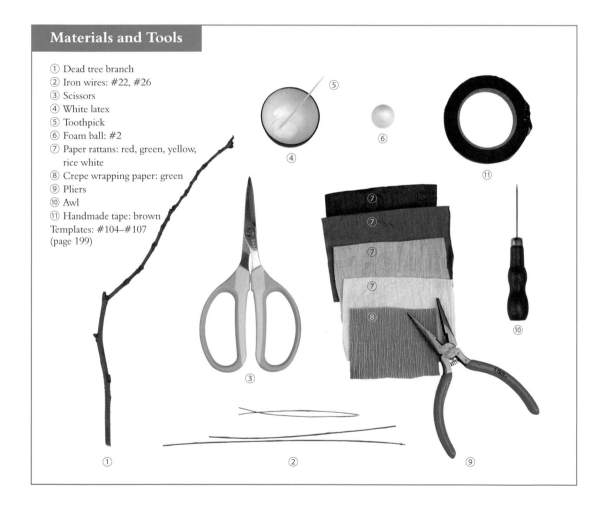

Materials and Tools

① Dead tree branch
② Iron wires: #22, #26
③ Scissors
④ White latex
⑤ Toothpick
⑥ Foam ball: #2
⑦ Paper rattans: red, green, yellow, rice white
⑧ Crepe wrapping paper: green
⑨ Pliers
⑩ Awl
⑪ Handmade tape: brown
Templates: #104–#107
(page 199)

How to Make It

1 Cut five to seven petals along the vertical veins of the red rattan paper based on the pattern #104 on page 199.

2 Wrap the petal around the head of the awl, and press it against the awl to produce some fine veins.

3 Make the petal look three-dimensional with your fingertips.

4 Cut a 6-centimeter strip out of the rice white rattan paper, apply white latex onto it, and fold it in half.

5 After the white latex dries up, cut dense and fine fringes on one edge of the strip.

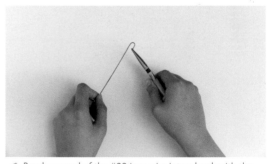

6 Bend one end of the #22 iron wire into a hook with the pliers.

7 Hook a small part of the paper strip and clamp the hook tightly with the pliers.

8 Apply white latex onto the bottom of the paper strip and wrap it around the hook to form the flower core.

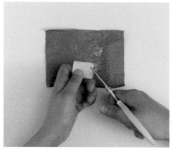

9 Cut the yellow rattan paper into fine scraps. Gather the scraps together for later use.

10 Apply white latex on top of the flower core.

11 Dab the top of the stamens with the yellow scraps in imitation of pollen.

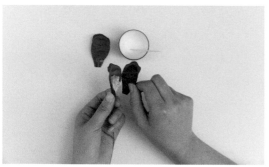

12 Apply white latex onto the bottom of the petals. Paste three petals evenly around the core.

13 Paste two to four petals in graceful disorder in the peripheral area.

14 Insert the #22 iron wire into the #2 foam ball.

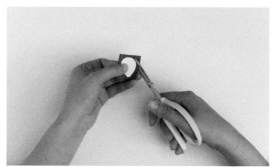

15 Cut the petals that can cover the bud based on the pattern #105 on page 199.

16 Follow steps 2 and 3 to treat the petals. Apply white latex to them and paste them around the foam ball.

17 Cut some calyxes out of the green crepe wrapping paper based on the pattern #107 on page 199.

18 Apply white latex onto the calyxes and paste them onto the lower halves of the flower and the bud.

19 The flower and bud are complete.

20 Cut two leaves for later use based on the pattern #106 on page 199.

21 Apply white latex onto one side of a leaf and place a #26 iron wire in its middle.

22 Paste the two leaves together face-to-face to form a complete leaf. Scrape some veins on it with your fingernail.

23 Make three leaves. Prepare to arrange these leaves.

24 Fasten the flower, the bud and the leaves one after another onto the dead tree branch with the brown tape.

25 A branch of camellia with Oriental charm is thus complete.

22. The Winter Sweet

The winter sweet is a traditional flower for appreciation specifically in China. It is as yellow as beeswax with intoxicating fragrance. As it blooms alone in the depth of winter against snow, it has been loved by scholars and men with a noble spirit and eulogized in poetry. Several branches of winter sweet in a vase placed on a table show the refined taste as well as self-restraint of the owner.

The language of the flower: noble-minded and faithful.

Dongzhi (Winter Solstice): December 21–23

Dongzhi is the 22nd solar term according to the 24 terms of the year. It is the day when the Northern Hemisphere is tilted the farthest from the sun, causing the daytime to become the shortest in the Northern Hemisphere. After that day, the daytime becomes longer as the sun moves northwards. Astronomically, this day marks the beginning of winter in the Northern Hemisphere. Since very few flowers bloom in winter, the winter sweet which flowers against severe cold adds luster to the Winter Solstice.

Materials and Tools

① Marker: brown
② Needle-nose pliers
③ Awl
④ Scissors
⑤ Handmade tapes: brown, yellow
⑥ Dead tree branch
⑦ Toothpick
⑧ White latex
⑨ Crepe wrapping paper: brown
⑩ Float-dye paper: yellow
⑪ Iron wires: #26
Templates: #14, #15
(page 184)

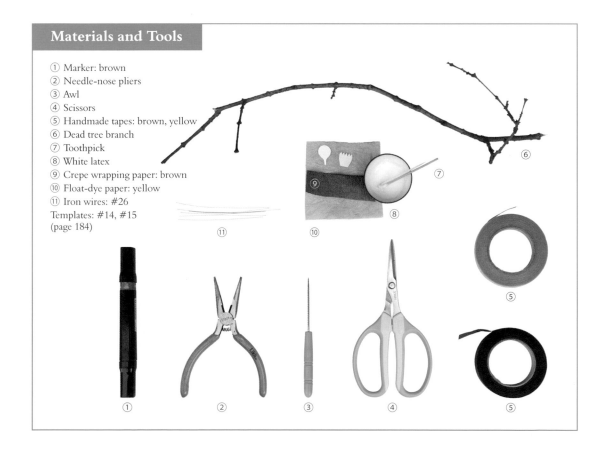

How to Make It

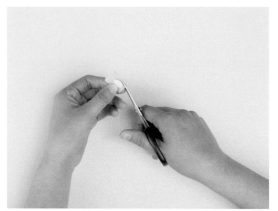

1 Cut some petals out of the yellow float-dye paper based on the pattern #14 on page 184.

2 Reel the petal tightly around the awl and press it against the awl handle before unfolding it, which gives the petal fine veins.

3 Make each petal bulge out in the middle with your finger pulp to create a three-dimensional effect.

4 Cut the yellow tape along the central line.

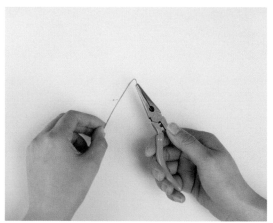

5 Bend a small hook on one end of the iron wire with the needle-nose pliers. Press the hook from both sides.

6 Wrap the hook with the yellow tape.

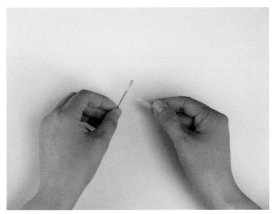

7 The hook thus looks like a cotton bud, which will serve as the flower core.

8 Repeat steps 5 to 7 using another iron wire. Wrap the hook again with the uncut yellow tape until the hook becomes round and as big as a soybean. This will serve as the flower bud.

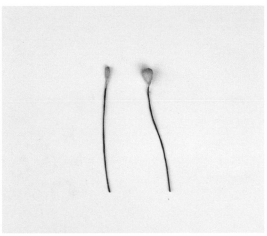

9 Make several cores and buds.

10 Paste the well-treated petals in step 3 around the surface of the flower core with white latex.

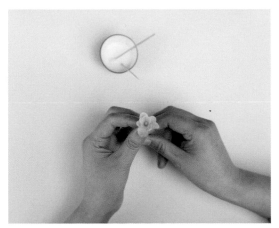

11 Paste two to three layers of petals from inside out.

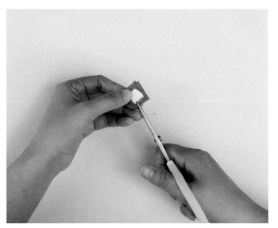

12 Draw level the brown crepe wrapping paper and cut the shape of the calyx out of it based on the pattern #15 on page 184.

13 Apply some white latex on one side of the calyx.

14 Wrap it at the bottom of the flower.

15 Use the brown marker to paint the calyx of the flower bud.

16 Prepare more buds and flowers of varied styles and sizes.

17 Wrap the flowers one by one onto the dead branch with the brown tape. Be careful not to expose the iron wire. Wrap it all with the tape.

18 A branch of winter sweet is thus complete.

23. The Chinese Narcissus

The narcissus is traditionally one of the famed flowers in China. With its refreshing fragrance, simple elegance, and unearthly beauty, it has shared the titles of Four Elegant Flowers with the orchid, chrysanthemum and calamus, and Four Friends in Snow with the plum, camellia and winter jasmine. Grown in a bowl of water on a table or window and supplemented with some small pebbles around it, the flower will display its beauty and charm to the fullest in the desolate winter, bringing in an atmosphere of warmth and auspiciousness. Therefore, it is often used for new-year celebrations. Yang Wanli (1127–1206), a poet in the Song Dynasty, wrote a poem eulogizing the narcissus, in which he compared the flower to the moon for simplicity and elegance and to fairies for purity and character.

The language of the flower: success in everything you do.

Xiaohan (Slight Cold): January 5–7

Xiaohan is the 23rd solar term according to the 24 terms of the year, meaning the coming of the coldest days in a year. This is when the narcissus is in full bloom. It is pure and noble, giving out faint and sweet fragrance.

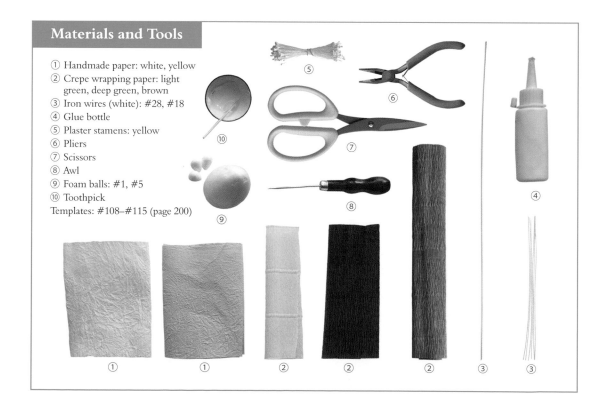

Materials and Tools

① Handmade paper: white, yellow
② Crepe wrapping paper: light green, deep green, brown
③ Iron wires (white): #28, #18
④ Glue bottle
⑤ Plaster stamens: yellow
⑥ Pliers
⑦ Scissors
⑧ Awl
⑨ Foam balls: #1, #5
⑩ Toothpick
Templates: #108–#115 (page 200)

① ① ② ② ② ③ ③

How to Make It

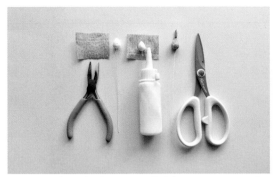

1 Secure the #1 bud onto an end of the #18 iron wire with the pliers. Cut a strip from the deep green crepe wrapping paper with the scissors, the size of which should be able to cover the bud completely. Apply white latex onto the strip and cover the bud with it. Twist both ends of the strip tightly and trim off the redundant crepe wrapping paper.

2 Make more buds with the light green crepe wrapping paper. Then cut some strips out of the green crepe wrapping paper, apply some white latex to them, and wrap them around the iron wires.

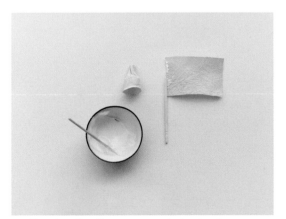

3 Take out two yellow stamens and fold them in half. Then wrap them with the #28 white iron wire, one stamen taller than the rest.

4 Apply some white latex onto the long strip cut out of the deep green crepe wrapping paper and wrap it around where the stamens and iron wire meet.

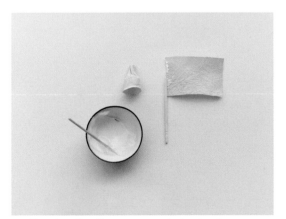

5 To make yellow flower core, cut the handmade paper based on the pattern #108 on page 200. Apply some white latex onto the shorter edge of the paper.

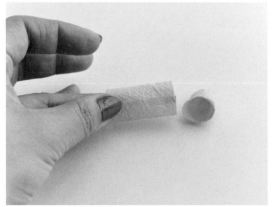

6 Place your finger inside the paper, and paste the edges to form a cylinder.

7 Pinch one end of the cylinder tightly, but do not paste it. This is the core of the flower.

8 Apply some white latex onto the crepe wrapping paper at the bottom of the stamen from step 4 and pass the stamen through the core.

9 Paste the bottom of the core and the stamen tightly together before the white latex dries.

10 Make more such combinations for later use.

11 Cut some petals of the narcissus out of the white handmade paper based on the pattern #109 on page 200.

12 Cut the #28 white iron wire into sections, apply some white latex to one end, and paste them in the center of the petals, leaving a space of about 2 millimeters on the top of the petals.

13 Scrape the top of the petal with the awl until it bends.

14 Both sides of the petal tip need to be scraped.

15 Make some more petals. Prepare to arrange the core and petals together with white latex.

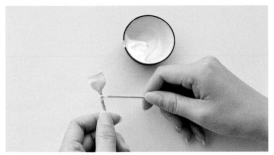

16 Apply some white latex to the bottom of the yellow flower core.

17 Paste the petals around the core. Each flower should consist of six petals, three above, three below; paste them together tightly.

18 Create some sharp points at the tip of the petals with your hands.

19 The bottom of the flower completed.

20 Cut leaf-like shapes out of the deep green crepe wrapping paper based on the patterns #113 to #115 on page 200 and scrape them with the awl until they bend.

21 Thicken the iron wire by wrapping the long strip cut out of the deep green crepe wrapping paper around it. Wrap the part at the bottom of the flower until it becomes olive-shaped.

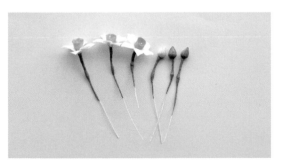

22 Wrap all the iron wire with a flower or bud with the deep green crepe wrapping paper until they become thicker.

23 Arrange the buds and flowers together in graceful disorder.

24 Secure them together with the deep green crepe wrapping paper and add to them the #18 iron wire.

25 Wrap the branch evenly with the deep green crepe wrapping paper and prepare to arrange the leaves.

26 Paste the leaves symmetrically onto the bottom of the branch.

27 Insert the bottom end of the iron wire into the #5 foam ball. Cut the shape of the husk that covers the foam ball out of the light green crepe wrapping paper based on the pattern #112 on page 200. Make the husk bulge out with your hand.

28 Wrap the white foam ball with the light green husk.

29 Prepare to make husks out of the brown crepe wrapping paper.

30 Pull open the elastic brown crepe wrapping paper. Tear the paper into some irregular shapes with fluffy edges. You can also refer to the pattern #111 on page 200.

31 Paste them outside the green husks and cover the white foam ball completely.

32 The linking parts below the flowers should also be pasted with green husks.

33 Cut some husks out of the deep green crepe wrapping paper based on the pattern #110 on page 200 and twist them into braids before unfolding them.

34 Apply white latex to two husks. Paste them face-to-face onto where the twigs meet in imitation of the rind of the narcissus.

35 A vivid-looking Chinese narcissus is thus complete.

24. The Moth Orchid

Graceful and beautiful, the moth orchid is known in China as Queen of Orchids. As it resembles a dancing butterfly, it is also named butterfly orchid. While the colored orchid exhibits unique dynamic beauty, the white one looks pure and noble.

The language of the flower: happiness descending quietly.

> ### *Dahan* (Great Cold): January 20–21
>
> *Dahan* is the last solar term according to the 24 terms of the year. By then, people are busy preparing for the Spring Festival, the most important festival in China. During the Spring Festival, the graceful moth orchid is the most common flower to decorate people's homes.

Materials and Tools

① Watercolor pen (brown)
② Colored pencils (green and yellow)
③ Pliers
④ Scissors
⑤ Iron wires: #26, #18
⑥ Double-headed rod
⑦ Glue bottle
⑧ Face tissue
⑨ Crepe wrapping paper: light green
⑩ Toothpick
⑪ Crumpled paper: dark green
⑫ Float-dye paper: white
⑬ Foam balls: #1, #2
Templates: #88–#91 (page 196)

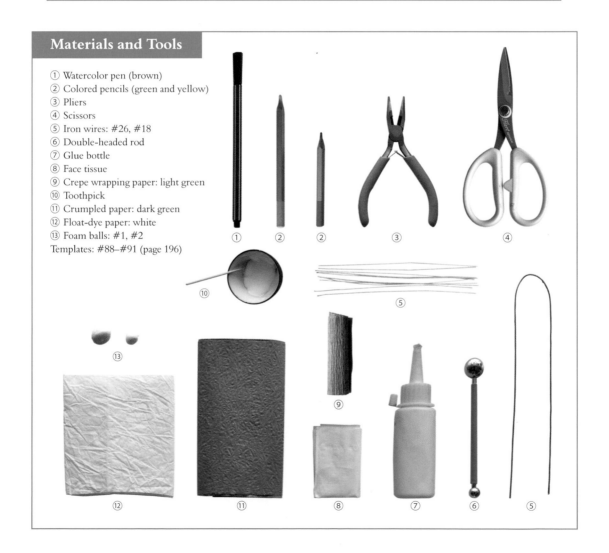

How to Make It

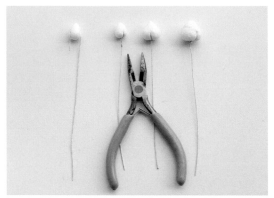

1 Secure the big and small foam balls firmly with the #26 iron wire and twist their bottoms tightly together with the pliers.

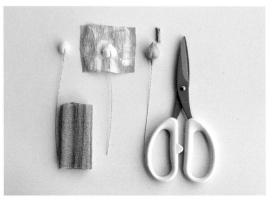

2 Cut rectangular strips out of the light green crepe wrapping paper based on the sizes of the foam balls. Apply white latex onto them and then wrap them around the foam balls. After pinching them tightly together, cut the redundant part. What is left is a flower bud.

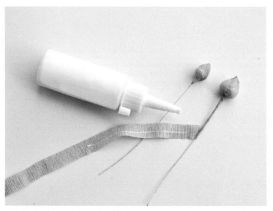

3 Cut a long strip out of the crepe wrapping paper, apply white latex to it, then wrap it around the iron wire with the bud on it.

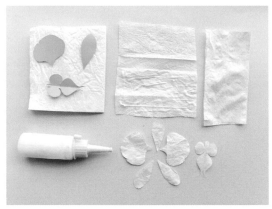

4 Glue a piece of the white float-dye paper and make it thicker by folding it in half. Cut six petals out of it based on the patterns #88 to #90 on page 196, two bigger petals, three smaller petals, and one irregular-shaped petal. You can make more petals for later use.

5 While waiting for the white latex to dry up, twist the bigger and smaller petals into braids to produce natural veins.

6 Unfold the petals again.

7 Scrape the edge of the bigger petal smooth with the back of the scissors. Make the edge wave-like with your fingers.

8 Scrape veins on the three smaller petals with your fingernail.

9 In the picture are bigger and smaller petals that have been completed.

10 Dab the bottoms of all the regular-shaped petals with the green pencil.

11 Paint the central part of the irregular-shaped petal yellow.

12 Paint other parts green. Make sure there is a change in the shade of the color.

13 Paint the other side green as well.

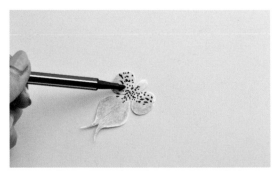

14 Finally, paint some dots of various sizes with the brown watercolor pen.

15 Fold some tissue paper together several times to make it thicker. Place the irregular-shaped petal on the tissue. Press the smaller head of the double-headed rod against the petal to produce a round curvature.

16 Make more curvatures by pressing the smaller head against all parts of the petal.

17 Finally, press the petal with the bigger head of the rod.

18 Six petals that have been completed.

19 Tear a long strip out of the face tissue, apply white latex to it, and wrap it around one end of a #26 iron wire to form the shape of the orchid core.

20 Pinch the core tightly. Apply white latex onto its surface after the white latex inside the face tissue dries up. Prepare to paste the petals.

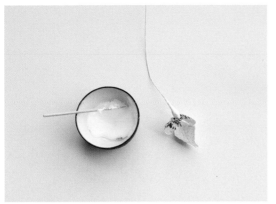

21 First, paste the irregular-shaped petal onto the core.

22 Then apply white latex to the bottoms of the two bigger petals.

23 Form a complete flower by arranging the six petals around the core as shown in the picture.

24 Repeat the above steps to make more flowers for later use, and wrap the #26 iron wires with the long strips cut out of the crepe wrapping paper. You can also make several raindrop-shaped buds this way: first, secure the foam balls with the iron wire, second, apply white latex onto the green crepe wrapping paper and wrap it around the foam balls, and lastly, trim the redundant crepe wrapping paper.

25 The completed buds and flowers.

26 Cut a rectangular strip out of the green crumpled paper. Apply white latex to half of the strip and then fold it in half. Cut the shape of a leaf out of the strip based on the pattern #91 on page 196 and scrape veins on the leaf with your fingernail.

27 Make two leaves.

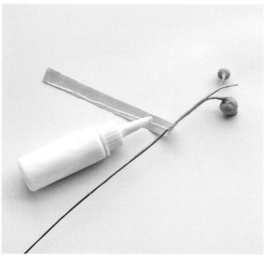

28 Apply white latex to the long strip cut out of the green crepe wrapping paper, and wrap the buds onto the #18 iron wire with it from top to bottom and from small to big.

29 Arrange the flowers in graceful disorder onto the iron wire.

30 Paste the two leaves symmetrically onto the iron wire. Wrap the iron wire evenly with crepe wrapping paper strips.

31 Sort out the work after all these are done. Make the petals face outside toward one direction.

32 Thus a branch of quietly elegant moth orchids is complete.

Acknowledgement

The editor invited us early last summer to write a book on the making of Chinese paper flowers, a book that would be both instantly understandable and also capable of presenting Oriental elements. We are particularly grateful to Cui Wei, who photographed every step during flower making, and to Zhu Zhu, who helped us design and photograph the finished works.

It took more than five months from the official signing of the publication contract to the completion of this book. I was afraid that I might not be able to make each and every flower and then design them all myself based on the characteristics of Chinese flower arrangement, since this would be both time- and energy-consuming. Fortunately, Ms. Yue Yunyun, my friend as well as teacher, agreed to work with me on this book. As we lived nearly 300 miles away from each other, we had to travel extensively, even during the Spring Festival, for face-to-face discussions about how this book should be written. We even thought of quitting when things were not going smoothly. However, through hard work and mutual encouragement, we have finally made it, and the final product is a testament to our 10 years' pursuit of the art of paper flower making.

As passionate lovers of handmade flowers, we sincerely hope that you as readers can also discover the pleasure, as well as beauty, of life from these works.

Fig. 24   Noble and romantic, the blue roses are most ideal for your beloved on your anniversaries.

Appendix

Templates

The templates are for your reference. You can copy them on a piece of blank paper, which can then be cut. There are four kinds of lines on the template: black solid lines (——), leaf vein lines (-----), fold lines (—··—··) and grey solid lines (——). The solid lines can be cut with a pair of scissors, the leaf vein lines can be scraped with your fingernail, and the fold lines are where folding should be made. The grey lines are midlines of leaves, where iron wires are usually put.

Fig. 25 Real or artificial? It's hard to tell. They make immortal those lives that could be ephemeral.

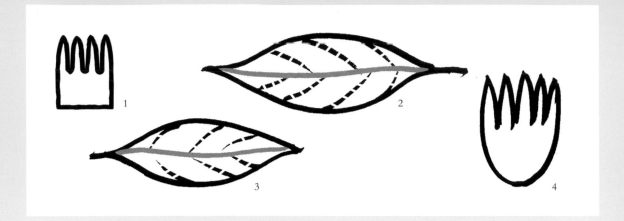

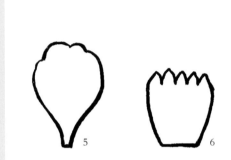

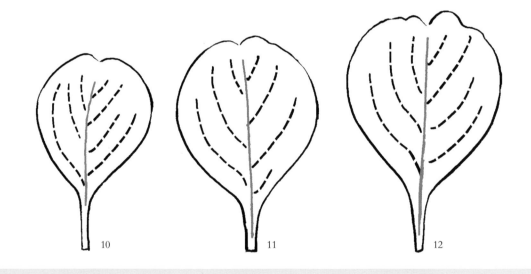

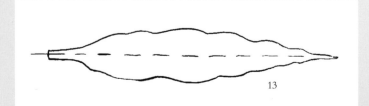

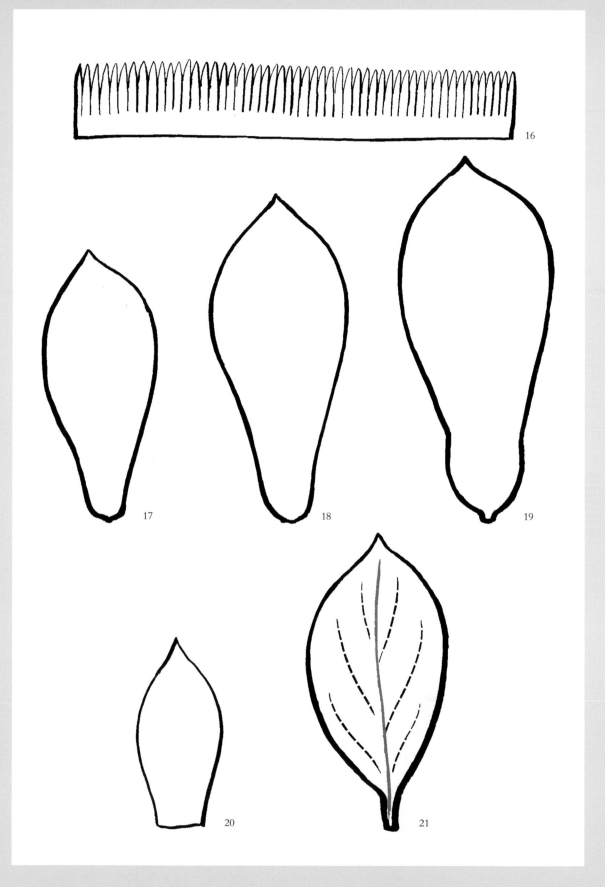

16

17

18

19

20

21

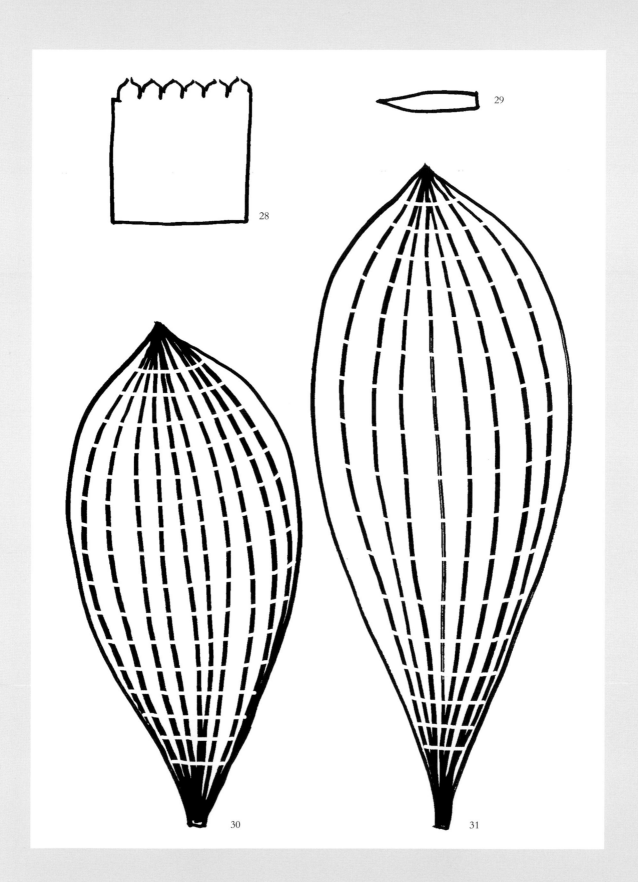

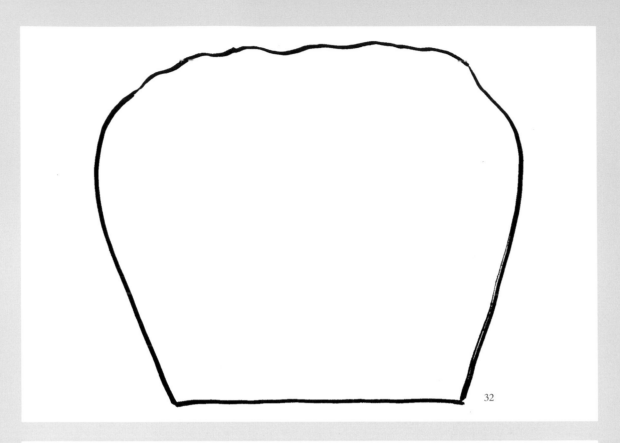

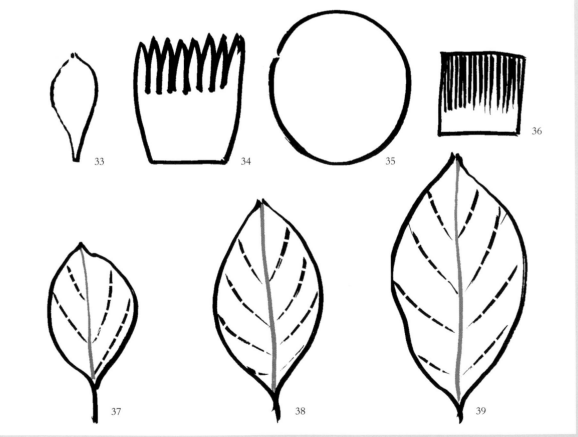

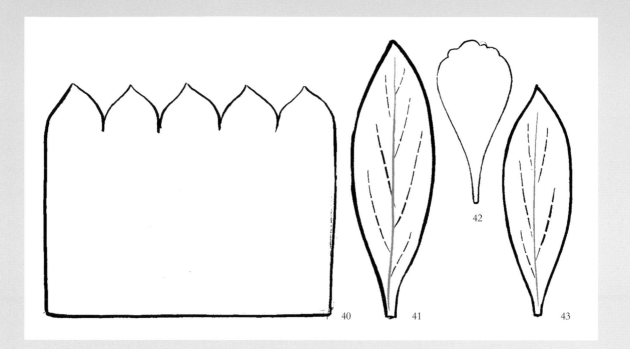

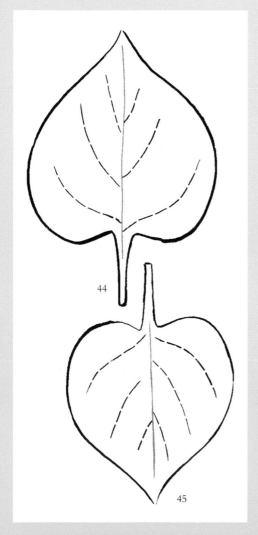

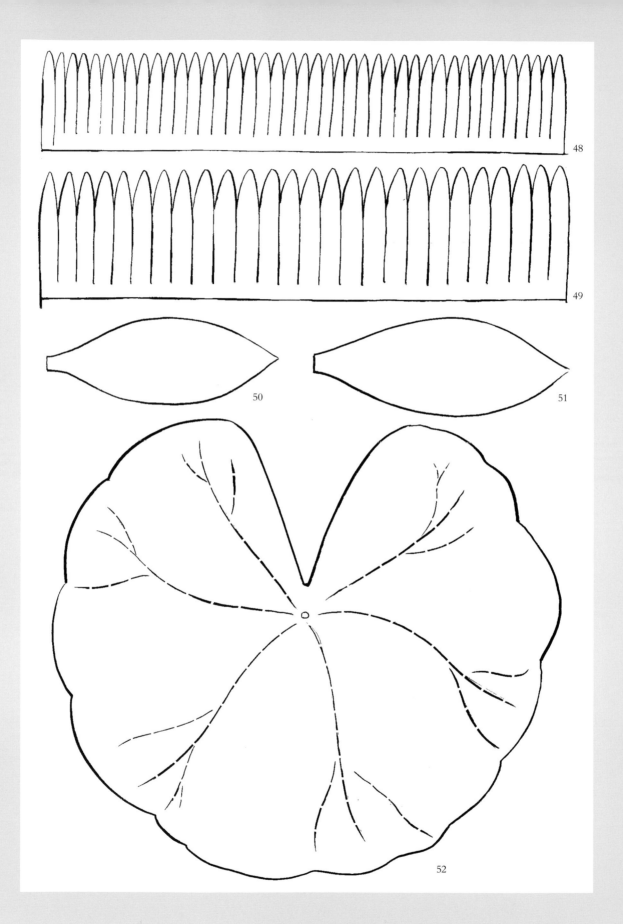

48

49

50

51

52

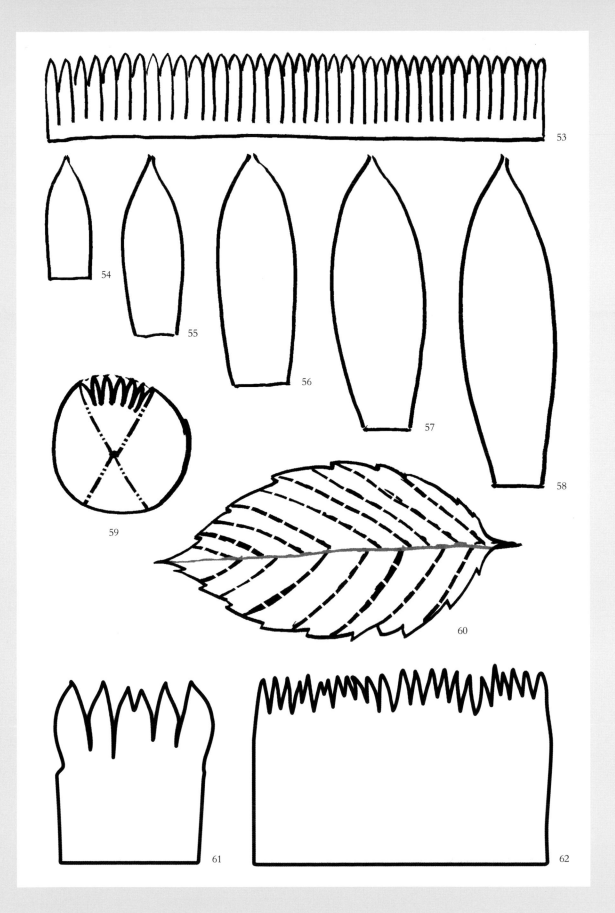

53

54

55

56

57

58

59

60

61

62

63

64

65

66

67

68

69

70

71

72   73   74

75   76   77

78   79

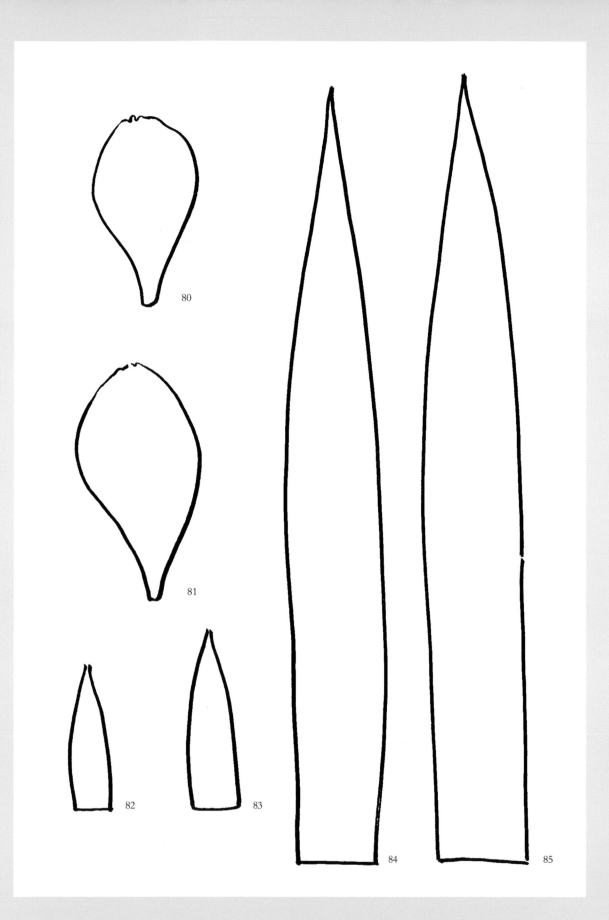

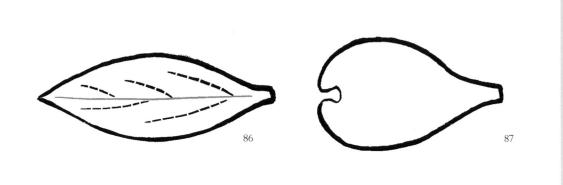

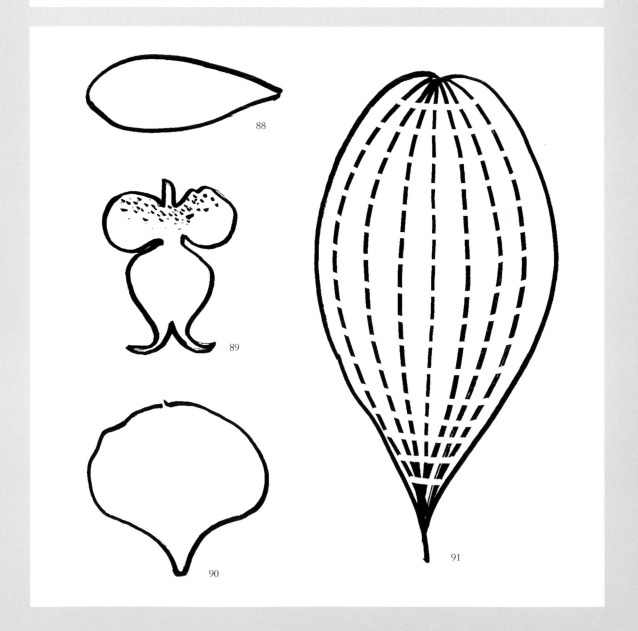

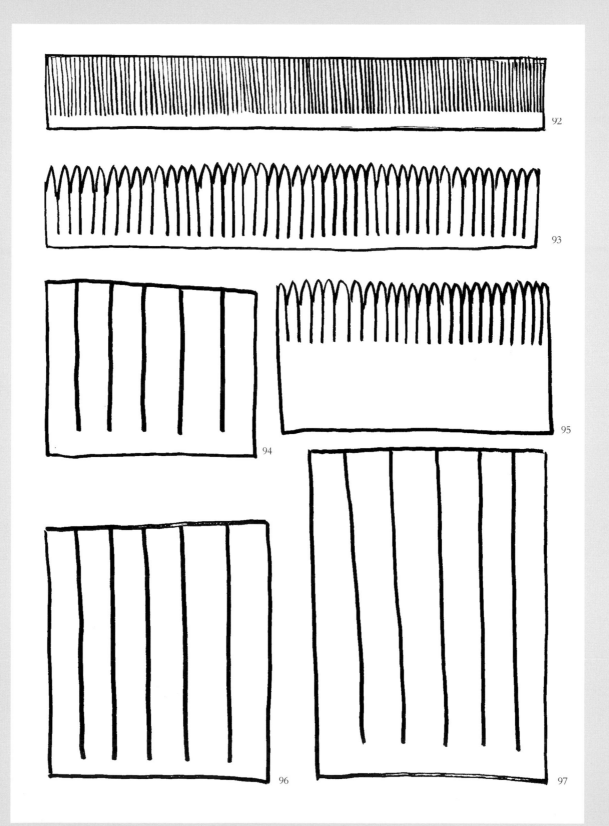

98

99

100

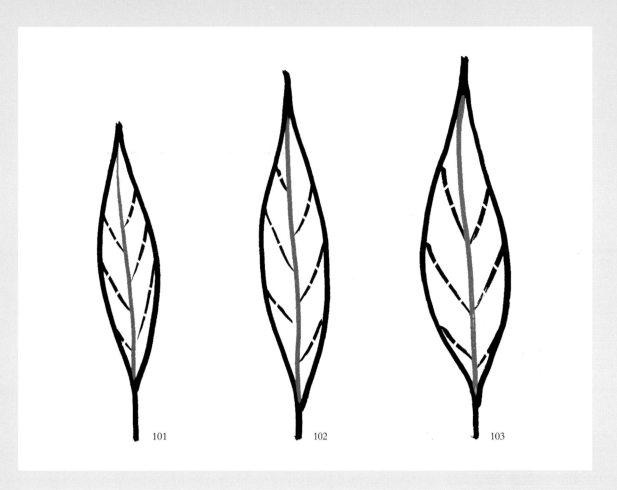

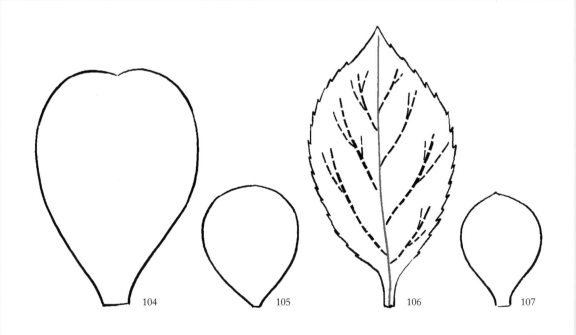

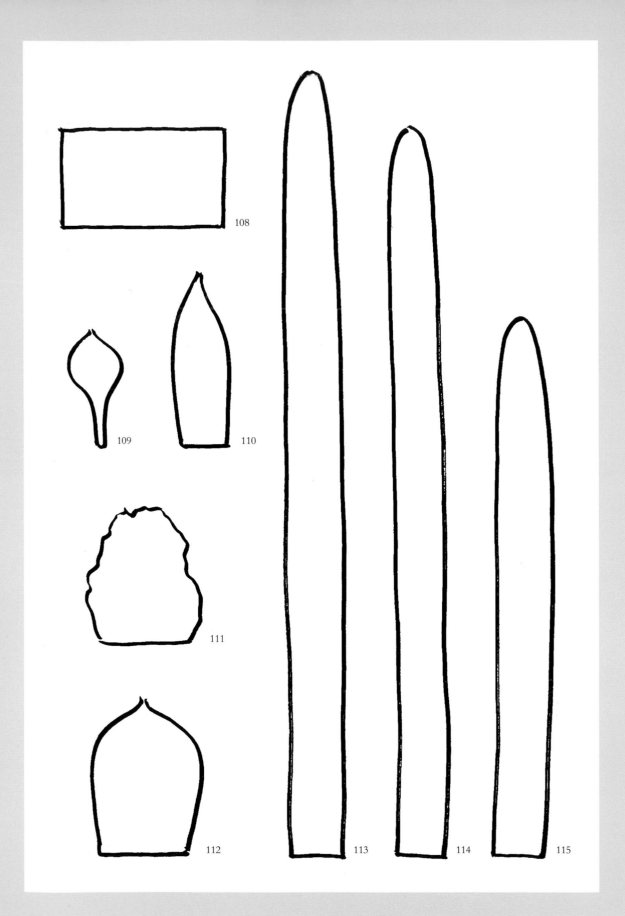

108

109

110

111

112

113

114

115